Java™ Development on PDAs

Java™ Development on PDAs

Building Applications for PocketPC and Palm Devices

Daryl Wilding-McBride

♦Addison-Wesley

Boston • San Francisco • New York • Toronto • Montreal
London • Munich • Paris • Madrid
Capetown • Sydney • Tokyo • Singapore • Mexico City

Many of the designations used by manufacturers and sellers to distinguish their products are claimed as trademarks. Where those designations appear in this book, and Addison-Wesley was aware of a trademark claim, the designations have been printed with initial capital letters or in all capitals.

The author and publisher have taken care in the preparation of this book, but make no expressed or implied warranty of any kind and assume no responsibility for errors or omissions. No liability is assumed for incidental or consequential damages in connection with or arising out of the use of the information or programs contained herein.

The publisher offers discounts on this book when ordered in quantity for bulk purchases and special sales. For more information, please contact:

U.S. Corporate and Government Sales
(800) 382-3419
corpsales@pearsontechgroup.com

For sales outside of the U.S., please contact:

International Sales
(317) 581-3793
international@pearsontechgroup.com

Visit Addison-Wesley on the Web: www.awprofessional.com

Library of Congress Cataloging-in-Publication Data

Wilding-McBride, Daryl.
  Java development on PDAs : building applications for PocketPC and Palm
devices / Daryl Wilding-McBride.
      p. cm.
    Includes index.
    ISBN 0-201-71954-1 (alk. paper)
    1. Java (Computer program language) 2. Application
software--Development. 3. Pocket computers. I. Title.

  QA76.73.J38W54 2003
  005.265--dc21

                                                2003050235

ISBN 0-201-71954-1
Text printed on recycled paper
1 2 3 4 5 6 7 8 9 10—CRS—0706050403
First printing, May 2003

Dedicated to Gemma and Liam, who hope that Daddy doesn't write another book for a while.

Contents

Preface

Java and PDAs are a powerful combination. Although PC sales have arguably peaked, PDAs are very much in a growth phase. In 2003, PDA sales should reach 19.5 million units and go on to reach 35 million units by 2005.[1]

Java is also a huge market, with millions of developers working world-wide in all areas of computing: from mainframes to matchbox-sized Web servers.

What This Book Is About

This book is about using Java to develop PDA applications. Having spent many years writing applications initially in C and later in C++, I felt that Java was a giant leap forward when I started using it in November 1995. I wrote this book because I wanted to develop applications for PDAs, but I did not want to go back to writing applications in C. After learning Java and realizing its power for developing a wide range of applications, I did not want to step back. Perhaps you feel the same way.

Aside from one's personal preference for any specific development language, there are numerous business reasons to use Java to develop PDA applications. First, your organization may be already using Java to develop enterprise systems. A large amount of time, money, and effort has probably been invested in building up Java expertise, tools, and resources.

Second, you may be attracted by the ability to write portable applications using Java 2, Micro Edition (J2ME). Just as Java code is portable across platforms supporting the other editions of Java 2 (Enterprise and Standard),

---

1. Source: Info Tech Trends, March 2002, `http://www.infotechtrends.com/pda_analysis.htm`.

applications written for J2ME are portable across platforms supporting the same configurations and profiles. However, it's fair to say that applications written for the Standard and Enterprise editions of Java 2 are more easily portable across platforms than applications written for the Micro edition. This is because, unlike the other editions, Micro edition applications target severely constrained devices. Because the platforms targeted by the Micro edition differ from each other in terms of memory and screen real estate much more than their enterprise and desktop counterparts, configurations and profiles dictate the features that are available on each platform. However, Micro edition applications that are written for one platform that supports a configuration and profile combination are quite portable to other platforms supporting the same combination. It's a nice feeling to know that an application written for J2ME on a PDA is usable on other devices supporting the same configuration and profile, and vice versa. This is vastly different from writing applications in C or C++ for the same devices. We'll be talking about configurations and profiles in subsequent chapters.

Third, you may wish to re-use simple business logic in your devices applications that has developed for other applications. You may want to check for a valid credit card number on the PDA application, and you may have a corporation-wide standard class for card number validation.

Any or all of these are good reasons to be interested in Java on PDAs.

Once you want to develop PDA applications using Java, you are faced with the secondary decision about which Java to use. There are several options. This book focusses on options that conform to the J2ME and PersonalJava standards because these are open standards for Java on resource-constrained devices. The standards are open because specifications are created as part of the Java Community Process, which is open to all developers for contributions and review of drafts.

Scope

The scope of the book includes developing Java applications for the Palm and PocketPC PDAs using J2ME and PersonalJava, respectively. Strictly speaking, PersonalJava is part of the Java 2 Standard Edition (J2SE) family rather than J2ME, but it is included in the book's scope because most PocketPCs come with PersonalJava installed. Additionally, as I write, implementations of the J2ME replacement for PersonalJava (the Personal Profile, which we will discuss in subsequent chapters) have not yet arrived for the PocketPC.

Although the applications presented in this book will run on other platforms, such as mobile phones, the specific intent is to focus on applications that run on PDAs and the considerations a PDA developer should keep in mind.

In the book, we will consider the end-to-end solution for integrating a PDA into the enterprise. As such, the book does include some server-side code.

Not included is coverage of other PDAs, such as the Sharp Zaurus. To make the book manageable, I decided to concentrate on the two dominant products in the PDA market. Also not included is coverage of PocketPCs running operating systems other than WindowsCE, such as iPaqs that run Linux.

The book does not cover Java-like languages for PDAs such as Waba, since they are not based on the open Java standard.

Audience

This book is written for developers who already know Java and who want to write Java applications for PDAs, in particular PocketPC and Palm devices. It is my intention to present the necessary concepts in practical terms, so that a Java developer can pick it up and start writing PDA applications in Java quite quickly. It assumes that you already have some Java experience with the Standard and/or the Enterprise editions.

This is not a book for people interested in learning Java. If that applies to you, I suggest buying an introductory Java book and downloading J2SE from java.sun.com. Learning Java with J2SE is a much better way to get started.

Conventions

Before we get started, I will explain some conventions followed in the book that hopefully make it easier to read and use.

Source code fragments, class and package names, and command-line interactions are displayed in a different typeface and appear like this.

Rather than bulking up this volume with page after page of source code listings, I have made the source code available for download from the book's companion Web site at www.javaonpdas.com. This allows me to ensure that the most up-to-date code is available. Likewise, I also prefer that the book is taken up with truly useful information. I hope you agree that this is a good idea.

The package naming convention in the source code uses a base name of com.javaonpdas, followed by a logical subgrouping based on the purpose of the class.

Development Environment

The chapters are intended to be independent of any particular development environment. In Chapter 3, "Setting Up the Development Environment," we discuss the options for a development environment. Whichever environment you initially choose, or to which you subsequently switch, the source code in other chapters will remain useful.

The development platform used in all the examples is Windows. This is not intended to imply that the examples will only work on Windows. The tools Ant, Tomcat, and Axis work on multiple platforms. The J2ME Wireless Toolkit from Sun is also available on Solaris and Linux, and the Palm OS Emulator is available on the Mac and Unix in addition to Windows. Generally, it is noted where tools run on other platforms, but I have not tried to run the tools on other platforms. I have tried to be platform-neutral as much as possible though, so if you are running a desktop operating system other than Windows the book is hopefully still useful to you.

Acknowledgments

I would like to thank Mike Hendrickson at Addison-Wesley, who was enthusiastic about my proposal for this book and decided to take it on. I am grateful to editors Julie Dinicola, Ross Venables, and Ann Sellers for getting me through the writting process and to the A-W production team—Marcy Barnes-Henrie, Scott Dissano, Jacquelyn Doucette, Rob Mauhar, and Sara Connell—for their patience in turning my manscript into a book.

I appreciate reviewers taking the time to read drafts of the manuscript and provide feedback. In particular, thanks to David Cittadini, David Cuka, Eric Freeman, Brad Jarvinen, Jacob Magun, Louis Mauget, Dan Podwall, and Michael Talley.

Thanks to Paul Manze at Insignia, who provided me some insights into Insignia's view of the PDA market.

Finally, while this book was conceived at about the same time as our second child, it ws a much longer labor. A special thanks to my wife Jasley, who supported me through the final push.

Daryl Wilding-McBride
April 2003

CHAPTER I

Java 2, Micro Edition: Configurations, Profiles, and Virtual Machines

This chapter discusses the J2ME standard and how it relates to PDAs.

J2ME is defined in terms of configurations and profiles. A configuration is a building block for basic functionality, whereas a profile builds on top of an existing configuration. Thus, a profile provides richer functionality that exploits the capabilities of the target device. Additionally, optional packages can be defined on top of profiles and configurations.

Figure 1.1 shows how configurations, profiles, and optional packages relate to each other. Each configuration may support one or more profiles. A configuration and a profile can have one or more optional packages.

There are two configurations currently defined in J2ME: the Connected Limited Device Configuration (CLDC) and the Connected Device Configuration (CDC). The CDC is intended for high-end PDAs, as well as other devices that have robust network connections and are reasonably powerful. The CLDC is intended for lower-end PDAs with intermittent network connections and are memory- and CPU-constrained.

Figure 1.2 shows the profiles defined for CDC and CLDC. The Personal Profile builds on the Foundation and Personal Basis profiles, which are supported by the CDC. The Mobile Information Device (MID) Profile extends the CLDC. In addition to the MID Profile, the optional packages Personal Information Management (PIM) and FileConnection also extend CLDC. The

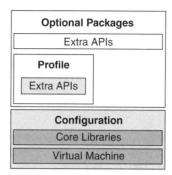

Figure 1.1   Optional packages, profiles, and configurations in J2ME

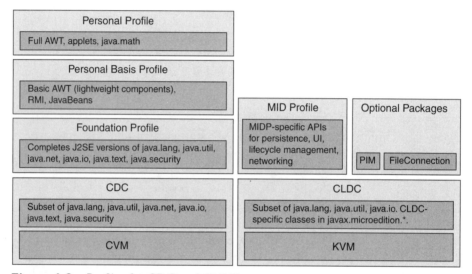

Figure 1.2   Profiles for CDC and CLDC

MID Profile, the PIM package, and the FileConnection package can be implemented independently on top of CLDC, and all three can coexist. These configurations, profiles, and optional packages are covered in more detail in subsequent sections.

J2ME Configurations

A configuration is a combination of a Java virtual machine and a collection of Application Programming Interfaces (APIs) that target a certain class of device. A configuration provides the basis for one or more profiles on a device. A profile is a set of APIs that enable functionality and take advantage of a more specific class of devices. A configuration defines a base set of APIs that must be implemented on all devices that support the configuration (which will target, for example, low-power devices with small amounts of memory). The profile sitting on top of the configuration must implement the configuration's APIs as well as APIs that are defined as part of the profile for that specific class of those devices (and the profile will target, say, PDAs).

It is important to note that the configuration specifies the capabilities of the underlying virtual machine, but it does not mandate a particular virtual machine. Vendors of profiles and their underlying configurations are free to provide their own virtual machine that conforms to the specification.

Connected Limited Device Configuration (CLDC)

The CLDC 1.0 was defined by JSR30 and released in May 2000. It targets devices with a set of basic characteristics. A CLDC device:

- is powered by batteries,
- has low processing resources,
- has low-speed ad hoc network connections,
- has 128 KB of memory available for the Java virtual machine and CLDC libraries, and
- has at least 32 KB available for the Java runtime and dynamic allocation of objects.

These characteristics define a wide variety of devices, including pagers, mobile phones, and PDAs. The CLDC defines a common basis for these devices in the following areas:

- Core Java packages
- Language features
- Virtual machine capabilities
- Networking and I/O
- Security
- Internationalization

It does not cover other areas that may be device-specific, such as the user interface, the application lifecycle, and event handling. These areas are covered by profiles.

The Java virtual machine providing the core of a CLDC adheres to the Java Virtual Machine Specification and the Java Language Specification, with some exceptions. With regard to the Java Language Specification, CLDC includes the following exceptions. Note that no profile or application on top of CLDC can require these things to be present.

- No floating point support (i.e., no floating point operations, no floating point literals, types, or values).
- No finalization.
- Although exceptions are supported, the number of error classes is limited.

With regard to the Java Virtual Machine Specification, the CLDC includes the following exceptions:

- No floating point support.
- No Java Native Interface (JNI).
- No user-defined class loaders.
- No reflection.
- No thread groups or daemon threads.
- No finalization.
- No weak references.
- Different classfile verification method (a two-phase approach featuring off-device pre-verification).
- Modified classfile format and class loading.

The CLDC inherits most of its classes from J2SE, and defines some CLDC-specific classes. The classes inherited from J2SE use the same class and package names. They include those listed in Appendix A, "Packages in CLDC," on page 207. Packages derived from J2SE use the J2SE names, whereas the CLDC-specific packages use the `javax.microedition` prefix.

The next version of CLDC was defined by JSR139, which was approved in March 2003.[1] The changes in CLDC 1.1 are summarized below:

- Floating point support has been added. The `Float` and `Double` classes have been added to `java.lang`, and some methods in other classes now allow for floating point values. Affected classes include `java.lang.Math`, `java.io.DataOutputStream`, `java.io.DataInputStream`, and `java.util.Random`.
- Some support for J2SE's weak references. The package `java.lang.ref` has been added.
- The `Calendar`, `Date`, and `TimeZone` classes in `java.util` are now more consistent with the J2SE versions.
- The `Error` class `java.lang.NoClassDefFoundError` has been added.

---

1. Java Specification Request (JSR) is a new specification (or a major change to an existing specification) for the Java platform. The process for the way in which JSRs are raised and developed is defined by the Java Community Process (JCP).

- Some minor, but useful, method additions to existing classes, such as the `intern()` method to the `java.lang.String` class, and the `toString()` method to the `java.util.Date` class.

The full CLDC 1.1 specification is available from `http://www.jcp.org/jsr/detail/139.jsp`.

Connected Device Configuration (CDC)

The CDC is a superset of CLDC. The CDC includes all APIs defined by the CLDC, including the `java.*` packages and the `javax.microedition.*` packages. CDC is designed for devices with more memory (2 MB of memory or more available to the Java platform) and better network connection (up to 9600 bps and beyond). CDC has a PersonalJava heritage, and so PersonalJava applications that do not use AWT (Abstract Window Toolkit). AWT should be quite portable to CDC (AWT capabilities are defined in CDC's profiles).

An implementation of the CDC must include full support for the Java Language Specification and the Java Virtual Machine Specification.

The packages of CDC are designed to be a complete set of APIs to support a virtual machine. They are taken from J2SE 1.3, with deprecated APIs removed. The resulting set of packages is as follows:

- `java.io`—including `BufferedReader`, `BufferedWriter`, `ObjectInputStream`, and `ObjectOutputStream`
- `java.lang`
- `java.lang.ref`
- `java.lang.reflect`
- `java.math`
- `java.net`—Classes from J2SE, including `URL`, `URLConnection`, `InetAddress`, and `SocketPermission`
- `java.security`—Encryption for object serialization. The following is not supported: secure code signing, certificates, keystore, Java Development Kit (JDK) 1.1 `Identity`, and `IdentityScope`.
- `java.security.cert`
- `java.text`—Minimal support for i18n
- `java.util`—Classes from J2SE, including `Array`, `BitSet`, `Calendar`, `LinkedList`, `Stack`, `Vector`
- `java.util.jar`
- `java.util.zip`
- `javax.microedition.io`

CDC implementations must support file input/output (I/O) (at least read-only) and datagrams.

CLDC Profiles

At this stage there is only one profile that overlays the CLDC: the MID Profile.

Although an implementation of MIDP was released for Palm devices by Sun in October 2001, it is really intended for smaller and more constrained devices, such as mobile phones and pagers. As such, it does serve as a common platform across a wide range of devices and the developer has the choice of a lower common denominator if the developer wishes to target those devices. To the user, it means that an application written for MIDP on a mobile phone will also work on Palm devices.

Mobile Information Device Profile (MIDP)

The MIDP specification defines additional requirements for the target device beyond the underlying CLDC requirements. Defined by JSR37, MIDP specifies that there must be an additional 128 KB of non-volatile memory for the MIDP components, 8 KB for persistent data created and used by applications, and 32 KB for the Java heap.

The MIDP 1.0 specification builds on the CLDC 1.0 and provides functionality in the following areas:

- Application lifecycle management
- User interface
- Persistent storage
- Networking
- Timers

MIDP does not cover the following areas:

- System-level APIs
- Application delivery, installation, and storage
- Security beyond what is already specified in the CLDC.

MIDP provides a few new classes in `java.lang`, `java.util`, and `javax.microedition.io`, and defines new packages for the user interface, persistent storage, and application lifecycle management extensions. These packages are named `javax.microedition.lcdui`, `javax.microedition.rms`, and `javax.microedition.midlet`, respectively. Appendix B, "Extensions of CLDC Provided by MIDP," on page 211, shows the new packages as well as the new classes in packages already defined in CLDC.

An MIDP application is called a MIDlet. A MIDlet is part of a group of MIDlets called a MIDlet suite. MIDlet suites can share resources, such as data persisted in a Record Management System (RMS) database on the device. An MIDP application must extend the class MIDlet and implement three of its methods that are defined as abstract: startApp, pauseApp, and destroyApp. These methods are called by the MIDlet application environment when the host environment requires the MIDlet to change state. A MIDlet has the following states:

- Paused. When the environment requires the MIDlet to enter the Paused state, it calls the pauseApp method to allow the MIDlet to release shared resources.
- Active. The MIDlet's startApp method is called after the MIDlet instance is created, and every time the MIDlet comes out of the Paused state.
- Destroyed. When the destroyApp method is called, the MIDlet is being notified that it should save its state and release any resources it was holding.

The developer can also cause the MIDlet to enter these states, using the methods notifyPaused, notifyDestroyed, and resumeRequest.

The following code shows a simple MIDlet, called SimplestMIDlet. This MIDlet displays a basic form, adds a command for pausing the MIDlet, and a command for exiting. In subsequent sections, we will add to this basic code to build up more interesting MIDlets.

```
package com.javaonpdas.introduction;

import javax.microedition.midlet.*;
import javax.microedition.lcdui.*;

public class SimplestMIDlet extends MIDlet
  implements CommandListener {

  protected Form mainForm = new Form("SimplestMIDlet");
  protected Command exitCommand =
    new Command("Exit", Command.EXIT, 1);
  protected Command pauseCommand =
    new Command("Pause", Command.SCREEN, 1);
  protected Display display = null;

  // In the constructor we add commands to the form, and tell
  // the form that this class will handle command events.
  public SimplestMIDlet() {
    mainForm.addCommand(exitCommand);
    mainForm.addCommand(pauseCommand);
    mainForm.setCommandListener(this);
  }

  // The startApp method is called when the MIDlet is created.
  public void startApp() {
```

```
    display = Display.getDisplay(this);
    display.setCurrent(mainForm);
    System.out.println("entered active state");
  }

  // The pauseApp method is called when the MIDlet enters the
  // paused state.
  public void pauseApp() {
    System.out.println("entered paused state");
  }

  // The destroyApp method is called when the MIDlet should save
  // its state and free any resources
  public void destroyApp(boolean unconditional) {
    System.out.println(
      "entered destroyed state (unconditional:" +
      unconditional + ")");
  }

  // The commandAction method is called when a command event
  // occurs
  public void commandAction(Command c, Displayable d) {
    if (c == exitCommand) {
      destroyApp(false);
      notifyDestroyed();
    }
    else if (c == pauseCommand) {
      // The developer can cause the MIDlet to enter paused
      // state by calling the notifyPaused method
      notifyPaused();
    }
  }
}
```

MIDP 2.0

MIDP 2.0 builds on MIDP 1.0, and is backward compatible with it, so that applications developed for MIDP 1.0 will also run on MIDP 2.0. Defined in JSR118, the final specification was released in November 2002. It assumes CLDC 1.0 functionality underneath, although it will also work with CLDC 1.1.

MIDP 2.0 adds some new packages:

- javax.microedition.lcdui.game. This package includes classes for creating a game environment. It includes a new GameCanvas and Sprites.

- `javax.microedition.media` and `javax.microedition.media.control`. MIDP 2.0 includes a subset of the Mobile Media API (JSR135) and supports tone generation and playback of sampled sound.
- `javax.microedition.pki`. Certificates for secure network connections.

To obtain a copy of the MIDP 2.0 specification, go to `http://www.jcp.org/jsr/detail/118.jsp`.

MIDP Implementations for PDAs

In this section, we have a look at several vendor's implementations of the MIDP specification for PDAs.[2]

Sun's MIDP for Palm

MIDP for Palm is an implementation of MIDP 1.0 and CLDC 1.0 for Palm OS 3.5.x. It includes a tool for converting a Java Archive (JAR)/Java Application Descriptor (JAD) pair produced with any MIDP Integrated Development Environment (IDE) into a Palm Resource File—a Palm application (PRC) for downloading to a Palm. It also includes the KVM and MIDP/CLDC libraries in a PRC package. KVM is the Java virtual machine underlying the CLDC configuration.

The hardware requirements for MIDP for Palm 1.0 are:

- Palm OS 3.5.x
- At least 600 KB free storage
- At least 4 MB total memory

Sun has tested MIDP for Palm on a Palm Vx, a Palm VIIx, a Palm IIIc, and a Handspring Visor Pro, but it should work on other Palm OS hardware as well, providing they meet the hardware requirements.

MIDP for Palm OS 1.0 is free and available for download from `http://java.sun.com/products/midp4palm/index.html`.

---

2. The test for a product to be included in this summary is: "Does the product include an implementation of MIDP specifically for PDAs? That is, does the tool produce a Palm OS executable?" All MIDP tools produce a JAD/JAR pair, but a Java PDA developer needs to produce a binary that can be downloaded to a PDA and executed.

IBM's WebSphere Studio Device Developer

IBM's WebSphere Studio Device Developer (WSDD, formerly VisualAge Micro Edition) is an IDE as well as a bundle of J2ME implementations (including CLDC and MIDP) for a wide range of embedded platforms and devices, including Palm devices. WSDD uses its own Java virtual machine, which is called J9. J9 has been ported to a number of embedded devices, including Palm devices. WSDD also offers the ability to call Palm OS native functions, but doing this is not consistent with the MIDP specification, and applications making use of native functions are not portable to other MIDP platforms.

The WebSphere Micro Environment includes an implementation of CLDC/MIDP for the Palm OS platform, using the Palm III, Palm Vx, and Palm V as a reference platform.

An evaluation version of WSDD is available for download from `http://www3.ibm.com/software/wireless/wsdd`.

esmertec's Jbed

JBed Micro Edition CLDC is a Java virtual machine and CLDC library for Palm devices and other platforms. The JBed virtual machine always compiles to native code, rather than interpreting bytecodes, which gives it a nice performance benefit. For more detail, see `http://www.esmertec.com/technology/jbed_me.shtm`.

Insignia Enhanced CLDC/MIDP

Insignia offers a CLDC/MIDP product based on its Dynamic Adaptive Compiler (DAC) technology. The compiler compiles commonly used blocks of bytecodes into native platform processor code, making execution much faster than an interpreter approach. Insignia quotes a 30 times speed improvement over the Sun MIDP reference implementation. The total executable footprint is 437 KB, based on the Pocket PC/ARM version.

CLDC Optional Packages

JSR075 (formerly the JSR for the PDA Profile specification) produced specifications for two optional packages that can be implemented on top of CLDC 1.0 or higher. They are the PIM and FileConnection optional packages. Even though they were defined by the same JSR, they can be implemented independently.

PIM Optional Package

The PIM optional package adds the package javax.microedition.pim to CLDC. The purpose of this package is to provide the developer with the ability to access and manage information in the PDA's address book, to do list, and calendar.

FileConnection Optional Package

The FileConnection optional package adds to CLDC 1.0 or higher the package javax.microedition.io.file. This package adds another connection type to the Generic Connection Framework (GCF), and provides access to the PDA's file system. The file system can be on the device itself, or on memory cards such as CompactFlash (CF) and Secure Digital (SD) cards.

CDC Profiles

Foundation Profile[3]

The Foundation Profile was developed by the JCP as JSR46.[4] Refer to the J2ME Foundation Specification for a definition of the APIs specified. It can be downloaded from http://java.sun.com/j2me/docs/.

An implementation of the Foundation Profile must support the protocols specified by the CDC, and in addition must support sockets and HTTP.

Personal Basis Profile

The Personal Basis Profile is intended for the interactive television and automotive markets. It targets applications where full support is required for a non-GUI application. It provides the capability for basic user interface presentation, but it is not intended to support applications requiring a heavy-weight GUI. The Personal Basis Profile provides support for the AWT light-weight components only.

Refer to the Personal Basis Programmer's Guide[5] for information on the differences between the Personal Basis Profile and the PersonalJava Application Environment. At a high level, the main differences are:

- PersonalJava targets the JDK 1.1.8, whereas the Personal Basis Profile targets JDK 1.3.

3. The discussion of the Foundation Profile refers to version 1.0a (May 29, 2002).
4. Refer to http://www.jcp.org/jsr/detail/46.jsp.
5. Refer to http://java.sun.com/j2me/docs/index.htm

- It was optional to include Remote Method Invocation (RMI) in Personal-Java. In the Personal Basis Profile, RMI is supported in an optional package.
- A number of deprecated APIs are not included in the Personal Basis Profile.

The Personal Basis Profile was developed by the JCP as JSR129.[6]

Personal Profile

The Personal Profile is the J2ME migration path for PersonalJava applications, and was developed by the JCP as JSR62.[7] To the Personal Basis Profile it adds Web fidelity and support for the legacy PersonalJava Application Environment. The Personal Profile is the CDC Profile that is intended for PDAs. Applications written to the Personal Profile APIs are upwardly compatible with J2SE JDK 1.3.

The Personal Profile is intended for applications that require full JDK 1.1 AWT support (that is, heavy-weight GUI components). It specifies three application models:

1. Applets. Standard JDK 1.1 applets.
2. Xlets. An Xlet is a lifecycle management interface. An application manager manages an Xlet through methods defined in this interface. The manager causes the Xlet to change state. The defined states are `Destroyed`, `Paused`, and `Active`.
3. Applications. Standard Java application, defined as a class with a `public static void main(String[])` method.

The Personal Profile adds to the Foundation Profile in these packages:

- `java.applet`
- `java.awt`
- `java.awt.color`
- `java.awt.datatransfer`
- `java.awt.event`
- `java.awt.image`
- `java.beans`
- `java.math`
- `java.rmi`
- `java.rmi.registry`
- `javax.microedition.xlet`
- `javax.microedition.xlet.ixc`

---

6. Refer to `http://www.jcp.org/jsr/detail/129.jsp`
7. Refer to `http://www.jcp.org/jsr/detail/62.jsp`

Differences between Personal Profile and JDK 1.3

The packages and classes of the Personal Profile are typically subsets of the JDK 1.3 packages and classes.

There is a small set of APIs in Personal Profile that have restrictions on their usage. They are:

- `java.awt.AlphaComposite`. Approximation of the SRC_OVER rule.
- `java.awt.Component`. The implementation may ignore a call to set the visible cursor.
- `java.awt.Dialog`. The implementation may limit the size, may prohibit resizing, may limit screen location, and may not support a visible title.
- `java.awt.Frame`. The same restrictions of Dialogs may also apply to Frames.
- `java.awt.Graphics2D`. Only instances of AlphaComposite may be used with setComposite().
- `java.awt.TextField`. An implementation may prohibit setting the echo character.

In each case, a system property will be set to `true` if the restriction is in place for the implementation being used. These system properties have the following keys:

- `java.awt.AlphaComposite.SRC_OVER.isRestricted`
- `java.awt.Component.setCursor.isRestricted`
- `java.awt.Dialog.setSize.isRestricted`
- `java.awt.Dialog.setResizable.isRestricted`
- `java.awt.Dialog.setLocation.isRestricted`
- `java.awt.Dialog.setTitle.isRestricted`
- `java.awt.Frame.setSize.isRestricted`
- `java.awt.Frame.setResizable.isRestricted`
- `java.awt.Frame.setLocation.isRestricted`
- `java.awt.Frame.setState.isRestricted`
- `java.awt.Frame.setTitle.isRestricted`
- `java.awt.TextField.setEchoChar.isRestricted`

Differences between Personal Profile and PersonalJava

PersonalJava was the original Java for high-end devices and embedded applications, but it will be superseded by the Personal Profile. The Personal Profile is a new definition, based on J2ME. When the designers of the Personal Profile started defining it, they started with JDK 1.3, removed all the deprecated APIs and all the APIs that they deemed unnecessary for modern mobile devices. PersonalJava is based on JDK 1.1 APIs.

Differences between PersonalJava and JDK 1.1.8

PersonalJava 1.2 inherits the APIs from JDK 1.1.8, slightly modifies many of them, makes some optional, and adds some specific to PersonalJava. It also inherits some APIs from Java 1.2 to support fine-grained access control and code signing. Portability of code without modification from JDK 1.1.8 to PersonalJava is therefore possible but is dependent on the specifics of the application.

As a practical guide to the similarities of PersonalJava and JDK 1.1.8, Appendix E, "JDK 1.1.8 Demonstrations on PersonalJava 1.2," on page 225 lists which of the demonstrations included with the JDK 1.1.8 work with PersonalJava 1.2.

Most of the cases in which the application does not work in PersonalJava are owing to differences in the security APIs. Recall that PersonalJava borrows fine-grained security APIs from Java 1.2 rather than JDK 1.1.8. However, there is a great deal of similarity between JDK 1.1.8 and PersonalJava 1.2, so that source code is largely portable between the two platforms.

Personal Profile Implementations for PDAs

Because the Personal Profile specification is relatively new, there are no implementations for PDAs yet available. Insignia has plans to release an implementation of the Personal Profile in the (northern) summer of 2003.

The IBM WebSphere Micro Environment implements CDC/Foundation, but it has no Personal Profile implementation as yet.

PersonalJava Implementations for PDAs

The Insignia Jeode product is an implementation of PersonalJava 1.2, and is available on a range of PDAs (see Table 2.3, "J2ME Implementations Available on PDAs," on page 19).

Summary

In this chapter we have delved into the configurations and profiles in J2ME, as well as some of the optional packages that add functionality to them. The J2ME architecture of configurations and profiles provides for growth over time by allowing new profiles and optional packages to add richer functionality, as the capability of devices increases.

In the next chapter, we will look at the implementations of Java available on different PDAs.

CHAPTER 2

Which PDA?

This chapter compares PDAs according to their strengths, weaknesses, and support for Java.

Why Choose?

As a Java developer, you probably think that having to choose a hardware platform is a concern of the past, inasmuch as Java runs on any platform. As we found in the previous chapter, that is not quite true for PDAs. There are portability issues between PocketPCs and Palm OS devices (because they run PersonalJava and MIDP, respectively). Although it is possible to structure your application so that common code can be shared between hardware platforms, the common code is likely to be limited to simple logic that can be separated from the user interface, persistence, and networking code. It is possible, but it will not be easy.

Therefore, you will probably want to choose which hardware platform you will target. The decision you make will affect whether you write a MIDP application or a PersonalJava application, which in turn may affect the amount of processing you do on the PDA and how much you need to do on the server.

The subsequent sections in this chapter are designed to help you make this decision.

Top Factors in Choosing a PDA for Java

In selecting a PDA platform for Java development, there are a number of factors that come into play. In consideration of these factors, it is important to remember that the two leading subclasses of PDAs—Palm OS devices and PocketPCs—are fundamentally different devices with quite different philosophies behind them. The major differences are listed in Table 2.1.

It is mainly owing to the differences in design philosophy that different J2ME configurations target the two types of device. Although Java will run on both devices, the richness of the Java platform varies, according to the capabilities of the device, and, accordingly, the configuration.

Cost

PocketPCs are generally more expensive than Palm OS devices. For the purpose of comparison, four top-end devices were selected of each type. The

Table 2.1   Differences in Philosophy

Palm OS Devices	PocketPCs
PIM heritage. The original Palm OS devices were basically high-end PIMs with larger screens and the ability to write rather than type.	PC heritage. The PocketPCs are basically miniature PCs.
Simple functionality. The Palm approach has been to do a few simple tasks very elegantly.	Rich functionality. The PocketPC approach has been to start with Windows and take functionality out, but leave a PC feel to the device. Hence, the Start menu and the file system remain the same.
Low processing power and long battery life. Palm OS devices have 20 MHz or 33 MHz CPUs, and typically 8 M of memory. The new ARM-based[a] Palm OS devices likely to appear in 2003 will match PocketPC speeds and memory capacity.	High processing power and shorter battery life. PocketPCs currently have 206 MHz or 400 MHz CPUs,[b] and typically 32 to 64 M of memory.

a. ARM is a processor used in many classes of device and is produced by ARM Ltd.

b. In comparing device speed, keep in mind that a 20 MHz device does not necessarily run applications 10 times slower than a device with a 200 MHz CPU, especially if the two devices have different hardware architectures, as do Palm devices and PocketPCs.

Table 2.2   A Sampling of PDA Prices (circa December 2002)

PocketPC	Low	High	Palm OS	Low	High
Casio E-200	$600	$650	Handspring Treo 270	$500	$700
HP iPaq 3970	$715	$780	Palm m515	$300	$400
Compaq iPaq 3870	$537	$680	Palm i705	$298	$450
Toshiba e740	$550	$600	Sony CLIE PEG-NR70V	$510	$600
Average	$601	$678	Average	$402	$538

street price was informally surveyed and compared. Table 2.2 lists the results in no particular order; prices are given in U.S. dollars.

From this selection of high-end PocketPC and Palm OS devices, we can see that PocketPC devices are roughly 25–50% more expensive than high-end Palm OS devices.

Corporate Standard

Whether you are an in-house developer targeting internal users, or a developer targeting the corporate market, corporate standards for PDAs will affect your choice of platform. According to the Winn Technology Group[1] (as of December 2002), the Palm OS has been chosen by 85% of the Fortune 1000 companies that have selected a standard handheld operating system.

Richness of Functionality

From a Java developer's perspective, the functional richness of the platform depends on whether you have access to it from Java. All PDAs have standard PIM functions (i.e., address books, notes, task lists, and calendars). The PIM optional package is designed to allow easy access to PIM functions of a PDA from Java. PersonalJava does not specifically have a PIM API, but it provides access to the functionality of the underlying operating system and application through JNI. However, the degree of accessibility through JNI depends on the availability of an API library to access the functionality.

---

1. Source: Top Ten Reasons to Choose a Palm Powered Handheld, 2002, http://www.palmsource.com/includes/top_ten_reasons_to_choose_palm_powered.pdf.

Richness of Java Support

The support for Java is important if you are a Java developer wanting to write applications for PDAs. Although PersonalJava is richer in Java APIs and closer to J2SE than MIDP and the CLDC optional packages, Personal-Java lacks the APIs to access PDA-specific features.

Wireless Support

Although both Palm OS and Pocket PC platforms are becoming wireless-enabled with WiFi and Bluetooth, the availability of these features to a Java application is limited. It will probably take some time for the Java APIs for wireless to emerge and mature, and then for vendors to add these APIs to their Java Virtual Machines (VMs) on PDAs.

Market Share—Actual and Trend

In the 1990's, Palm OS was the dominant PDA operating system in the market. Since that time, through several iterations of its offering, Microsoft has challenged that dominance and has been reasonably successful. In 2002, Pocket PCs were a strong alternative and growing in market share.[2] Figure 2.1

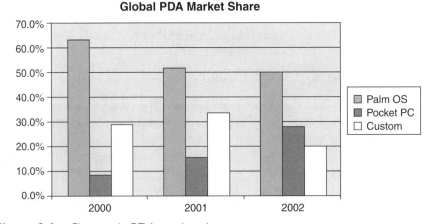

Figure 2.1   Changes in PDA market share

---

2. Sources: `http://zdnet.com.com/2100-1103-836270.html` and `http://zdnet.com.com/2100-1103-948358.html`.

shows the change in market share over a three-year period. The trend in that time has been that PocketPC has increased share, whereas Palm devices have decreased share.

Direction—Where Will the Vendor Be in Two Years?

With most PDA vendors likely to have released new models based on the Intel XScale CPU by the time this book is published, soon the hardware difference between Palm OS–based devices and PocketPC–based devices will have diminished. Palm OS 5 is visually and functionally similar to previous versions, although the memory constraints of previous Palm OS versions have been lifted.

Which Java on Which PDA?

Broadly speaking, PersonalJava is available on PocketPC devices, whereas MIDP is available on Palm OS devices. Table 2.3 shows the J2ME implementations currently available. PersonalJava is included in the table even though it is not strictly a J2ME implementation, but it is available on almost every PocketPC device.

Table 2.3 J2ME Implementations Available on PDAs

Operating System	CPU	Device	Java	Product
PocketPC 2002	StrongARM	HP iPaq 3800 series	PersonalJava 1.2	Insignia Jeode PDA Edition
PocketPC 2002	Intel XScale	Toshiba GENIO e550G	PersonalJava 1.2	Insignia Jeode PDA Edition
Lineo's Embedix Linux	StrongARM	Sharp Zaurus SL-5500	PersonalJava 1.2	Insignia Jeode PDA Edition
Windows CE 3.0	StrongARM	HHP Dolphin 7400	PersonalJava 1.2	Insignia Jeode PDA Edition
PocketPC 2002	StrongARM	NEC PocketGear	PersonalJava 1.2	Insignia Jeode PDA Edition

(continued)

Table 2.3   J2ME Implementations Available on PDAs *(Continued)*

Operating System	CPU	Device	Java	Product
Windows CE 3.0	StrongARM	Samsung NEXiO S150	PersonalJava 1.2	Insignia Jeode PDA Edition
PocketPC 2002	Intel XScale	Fujitsu Pocket LOOX	PersonalJava 1.2	Insignia Jeode PDA Edition
PocketPC 2002	StrongARM	Compaq iPaq as a reference platform	CDC/Foundation 1.0	IBM WebSphere Micro Environment
PocketPC 2002	StrongARM	Compaq iPaq as a reference platform	CLDC/MIDP 1.0	IBM WebSphere Micro Environment
Palm OS	68K	Palm III, Palm V, Palm Vx as a reference platform	CLDC/MIDP 1.0	IBM WebSphere Micro Environment
Palm OS	68K	Various	CLDC/MIDP 1.0	Esmertec Micro Edition CLDC
Palm OS 3.5.x	68 K	Various; capable of running 3.5.x (refer to Table 2.4)	CLDC/MIDP 1.0	MIDP for Palm OS 1.0
Windows CE 2.11	MIPS or SH3	IBM Workpad Z50, Compaq Aero 2100, HP Jornada 430 SE, and others	PersonalJava 1.1.3	Sun Personal-Java Runtime Environment for Windows CE 2.11 Version 1.0

Palm Models

As the Palm platform has evolved, the hardware has evolved as well. Additionally, new hardware vendors have developed non-Palm PDAs that run Palm OS. Table 2.4 shows a selection of devices produced by Palm Inc. and licensees of Palm OS.

Table 2.4 Comparison of Palm OS–Based Devices[a]

Device	Total RAM	Dynamic Heap[b]	Palm OS[c]	CPU Type	CPU Speed
Palm IIIx	4 MB	128 KB	3.1	Dragonball EZ	16 MHz
Palm V	2 MB	128 KB	3.1	Dragonball EZ	16 MHz
Palm VII	2 MB	128 KB	3.2.0/ 3.2.5	Dragonball/ Dragonball EZ	16 MHz
Palm VIIx	8 MB	256 KB	3.5	Dragonball EZ	20 MHz
Palm i705	8 MB		4.1		
Handspring Visor	2 MB	128 KB	3.1	Dragonball EZ	16 MHz
Handspring Visor Edge	8 MB	256 KB	3.5.2	Dragonball VZ	33 MHz
IBM WorkPad (Original)	4 MB	96 KB	3.0	Dragonball EZ	16 MHz
Qualcomm pdQ 1900	2 MB	128 KB	3.02	Dragonball EZ	16 MHz
Sony CLIE PEG-S500c	8 MB	256 KB	3.5	Dragonball EZ	20 MHz
Supra eKey	2 MB	128 KB	3.1	Dragonball EZ	16 MHz
Symbol SPT1740	2/4/8 MB	128 KB	3.2	Dragonball	16 MHz
TRG TRGpro	8 MB	128 KB/ 256 KB	3.3/ 3.5.1	Dragonball EZ	16 MHz

a. This list was derived from `http://www.palmos.com/dev/tech/hardware/compare.html`.

b. Depends on the version of Palm OS installed.

c. Palm OS version refers to the version originally shipped. Palm OS version of a particular device may have changed owing to upgrades.

Summary

In this chapter, we have covered some of the Palm and PocketPC PDAs available, which Java runs on them, and other factors to consider when targeting a PDA platform with a Java application. As the tables presented show, MIDP and PersonalJava cover most of the PDAs on the market, so the developer equipped with skills in these implementations can be confident of their market coverage.

CHAPTER 3

Setting Up the Development Environment

In this chapter we will walk through the steps involved in setting up the development environment for development of PDA applications using Java. The tools we will use in the book's examples are available for little or no cost. In the following chapters we will not be using any of the commercial IDEs. There are several reasons for this:

- Learning software development on a new platform is better at the lowest possible level. If you use a fancy IDE, often the tools will hide the lower level detail and you will not know how things work. You can always move to an IDE later, once you understand the underlying mechanics of building software for the new platform.
- It is often possible to do things that are not always possible to do with a higher-level tool or an IDE.
- The objective of this book is to show how anyone can develop Java applications for PDAs. Expensive tools are not required.

The tools we use in the following chapters are:

- Ant. Apache Ant (`http://jakarta.apache.org/ant/index.html`) is a very powerful, open-source build tool. Download the latest ZIP file and unzip it into a convenient location. This book uses Ant 1.5.

- A text editor, such as TextPad (`http://www.textpad.com/`). The text editor should preferably have highlighting for Java and XML syntax so that source code is easy to read.
- Java SDK (`http://java.sun.com/j2se/downloads.html`). We will use 1.1.8 (for compiling PersonalJava source code) and 1.4 (for everything else).
- Palm Emulator (`http://www.palmos.com/dev/tools/emulator/`).
- Sun's J2ME Wireless Toolkit (`http://java.sun.com/products/j2mewtoolkit/download.html`).
- Sun's MIDP for Palm (`http://java.sun.com/products/midp4palm/index.html`). Although it is free to download for personal development purposes, note that MIDP for Palm is not free to distribute commercially.

Installing the Book's Source Code

The source code for the book is contained in the ZIP file `JavaOnPDAs.zip`. The latest version can be downloaded from `http://www.javaonpdas.com`. The ZIP file contains the following:

- Ant build file `build.xml`. The build file describes how to build all the sample code, and includes useful tasks for starting and testing applications for Palm devices and PocketPC, as well as the server processes.
- Source code for Palm devices, PocketPC, and desktop applications.
- Pre-verified class files for Palm device source code.
- Palm `.prc` files for Palm device applications.
- HTML files used in Chapter 7, "Networking."

Unzip the ZIP file to a convenient location, preserving the directory structure. We will refer to this location as `${javaonpdas-base}`. The Ant build file does not assume the path for the base directory, but it does assume that the directory structure underneath the base directory is preserved.

The structure is shown in Figure 3.1.

The Ant build file includes instructions for the following:

- Compiling the desktop (i.e., server), PocketPC, and Palm device source code.
- Building a JAR for deployment to the PocketPC.
- Preverifying Palm device classes.
- Unjaring any external JARs for bundling into a single Palm device JAR.
- Building a Palm device JAR and updating a JAD file.
- Creating a Palm device PRC file.
- Running Palm device applications on the Palm emulator.
- Deploying and undeploying Web services on the server.

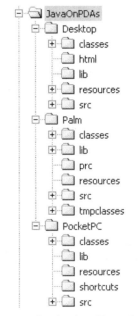

Figure 3.1   Directory structure for the book's code

- Running test clients.
- Running test tools.
- Creating PocketPC shortcuts for the Jeode PersonalJava JVM.

Setting Up the Palm OS Emulator

The Palm OS Emulator (POSE) is an essential part of your PDA Java developer's toolkit. Rather than download an application to a Palm device for testing, testing can be done on the POSE. This means that the edit-test-fix cycle is much faster.

The POSE is available for Windows, MacOS, and Unix. You will also need a Palm ROM to load into POSE. A ROM can be uploaded from a Palm device, or a ROM file can be licensed from Palm. If you live in the U.S., you can join the Palm OS Developer Program and gain access to ROM images immediately. If you live outside the U.S., you need to download an application form and send it to Palm.

When Palm has processed the license agreement, they will send you a username and password for accessing the Resource Pavilion and downloadable

ROM images. Point your browser to `http://www.palmos.com/dev/programs/` `pdp/login.html` and log on. The ROMs are packaged according to the Palm OS version and language. Download the appropriate ZIP file and unzip it into a convenient location.

Start the Palm OS emulator, and a screen similar to the one shown in Figure 3.2 will be displayed. Select New to create a new POSE session, and, as shown in Figure 3.3, select the ROM file you have just downloaded. Click on OK and the POSE should start up an emulated Palm session (see Figure 3.4).

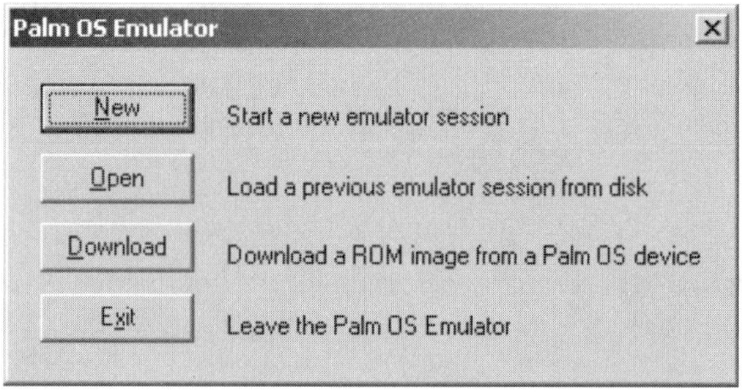

Figure 3.2   Creating a new POSE session

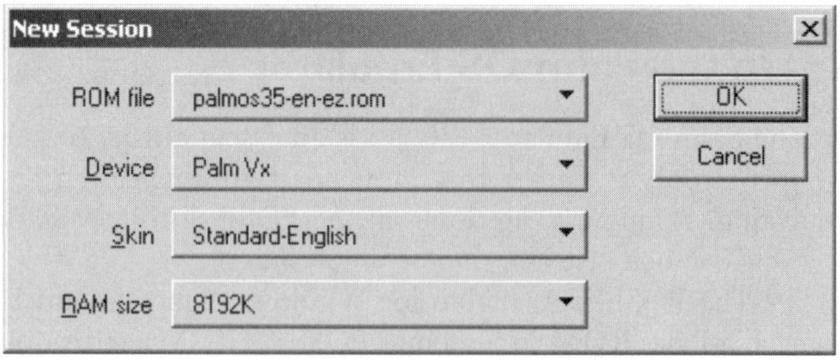

Figure 3.3   Choosing a ROM and device for the session

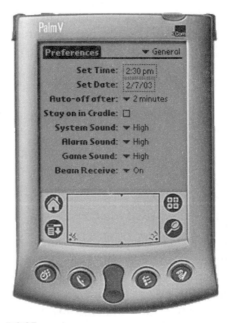

Figure 3.4   A new POSE session

J2ME Wireless Toolkit

Sun's J2ME Wireless Toolkit (J2MEWTK) is a set of tools for developing applications for the CLDC/MIDP platform. It runs on Windows, Solaris, and Linux, and provides an emulation environment for a variety of devices. It also uses the POSE to emulate the Palm device. The J2MEWTK allows the use of any text editor for editing source files.

The Java virtual machine provided with the J2MEWTK is the KVM, a compact virtual machine targeting devices with less than a megabyte of memory. Refer to `http://java.sun.com/products/cldc/wp/KVMwp.pdf` for more information about the KVM.

Download the Wireless Toolkit and install it in the default installation directory.

MIDP for Palm OS

Whether or not you decide to use Sun's J2MEWTK for the IDE in your development projects, if you choose a generic MIDP development toolset then you will also need a way to convert the MIDP JAD/JAR to a PRC for the Palm device. MIDP for Palm is a free graphical tool from Sun for doing just that.[1]

Included in the MIDP for Palm toolset:

- A utility for converting a standard MIDP JAD/JAR into a Palm PRC for downloading to the device.
- An implementation of KVM and the CLDC/MIDP libraries for the Palm.
- Some example Java applications.

MIDP for Palm takes up about 590 KB of memory and runs on devices that:

- Run Palm OS 3.5.x.
- Have at least 4 MB of total memory.

MIDP for Palm also includes an ability to capture output streams System.out and System.err.

Download the MIDP for the Palm ZIP file and unzip it into a convenient location. Install the Java runtime on the Palm by installing the MIDP.prc file from the MIDP for Palm PRCfiles directory.

Running Java Applications on the Palm Devices

This book uses MIDP 1.0 for developing Java applications on the Palm. To compile Java source code to deploy on the Palm devices, we need to go through a few simple steps. First, we compile the Palm source code using a Java 1.1 compiler (since MIDP and CLDC are based on Java 1.1 bytecodes). The CompilePalm Ant build target performs this step.

```
<target name="CompilePalm" depends="CompileDesktop">
  <!-- Compile the Palm source code -->
  <javac srcdir="${palmsource}"
    target="1.1"
    bootclasspath="${wtk-base}\lib\midpapi.zip"
    destdir="${palmunverified}"
    fork="true"
    executable="${jdk-base}\bin\javac"
```

---

1. The J2MEWTK also includes this functionality, but it does not include MIDP for Palm. The J2MEWTK produces a JAD file and converts to a PRC only when the application is run with the Palm emulator. A JAD is a parameter file for defining values of predefined MIDlet parameter values, and for user-defined parameters. The MIDP for Palm converter tool allows the developer to convert any JAD/JAR pair into a PRC.

```
        compiler="javac1.1">
        <classpath>
          <pathelement path="${palmunverified}"/>
          <pathelement path="${palmverified}"/>
          <pathelement location="${palmlib}\${palmsoaplib}"/>
        </classpath>
      </javac>
    </target>
```

This target compiles the Java source code and puts the resulting class files into a special directory. Because with the KVM verification is a two-part process, the first part of which is done on the desktop (and is called "preverification") rather than the device, the class files just produced must be preverified. This is done by the PreverifyPalm Ant build target.

```
    <target name="PreverifyPalm" depends="CompilePalm">
      <!-- Preverify the Palm classes -->
      <exec dir=".\" executable="${wtk-base}\bin\preverify.exe"
        failonerror="true">
        <arg line="-classpath
          ${wtk-base}\lib\midpapi.zip;${palmlib}\${palmsoaplib}
          -d ${palmverified} ${palmunverified}"/>
      </exec>
    </target>
```

This process takes the unverified class files from ${palmunverified}, verifies them using the preverification tool from the J2ME Wireless Toolkit, and puts the output class files into ${palmverified}.

The application may make use of external class libraries that may be supplied as JAR files. In this case, the Ant build target UnjarExternalLibraries unbundles the JARs into class files and puts them into the ${palmunjar} directory. This is done so that we can produce a single JAR file for deploying to the Palm.

```
    <target name="UnjarExternalLibraries" depends="PreverifyPalm">
      <unjar dest="${palmunjar}">
        <patternset>
          <include name="**/*.class"/>
        </patternset>
        <fileset dir="${palmlib}">
          <include name="**/*.jar"/>
        </fileset>
      </unjar>
    </target>
```

Now we are ready to create the Palm JAR. To create the JAR file we need a special manifest file that describes the MIDlet application. The manifest file describes:

- The application's name, the icon file to use, and the class name of the application.
- Vendor and version information.
- The J2ME version required.

The manifest below is from one of the applications we will be building in a subsequent chapter.

```
MIDlet-1: SOAPClient, ,↵
com.javaonpdas.webservices.clients.wingfoot.SOAPClient
MIDlet-Name: SOAPClient
MIDlet-Vendor: Daryl Wilding-McBride
MIDlet-Version: 1.0
MicroEdition-Configuration: CLDC-1.0
MicroEdition-Profile: MIDP-1.0
```

The Ant build target SOAPClientJAR is an example target that builds a JAR.

```
<target name="SOAPClientJAR" depends="UnjarExternalLibraries">
  <jar destfile="${palmverified}\SOAPClient.jar"
      manifest="${palmresources}\SOAPClient-manifest.txt">
    <fileset dir="${palmverified}"
      includes="com\javaonpdas\webservices\clients\wingfoot/↵
*.class com\javaonpdas\*.class"
    />
    <fileset dir="${palmunjar}"
      includes="**/*.class"
    />
    <fileset dir="${palmresources}"
      includes="**/*.png"
    />
  </jar>
  <updatejad jad="${palmresources}\SOAPClient.jad"
      relativePath="true" />
</target>
```

This target also updates the JAD file. The JAD file describes the MIDP deployment package.

```
MIDlet-Version: 1.0
MIDlet-Vendor: Daryl Wilding-McBride
MIDlet-Jar-URL: ../classes/SOAPClient.jar
```

```
MIDlet-Jar-Size: 42726
MIDlet-Name: SOAPClient
```

The JAD file can be prepared prior to the JAR file being built, but the `MIDlet-Jar-Size` item must be populated after the JAR is present. This requirement is addressed by a special Ant task called `updatejad` (see `http://www.stampy-soft.com/`). `updatejad` updates the JAR file size entry in the JAD file.

Now that we have a JAR and JAD pair, we can create the PRC for downloading to the Palm device. An example of a build target that performs this task is `SOAPClientPRC`.

```
<target name="SOAPClientPRC" depends="SOAPClientJAR">
  <java
  classname="com.sun.midp.palm.database.MakeMIDPApp"
  dir="."
  fork="true"
  failonerror="true">
  <classpath>
      <pathelement location="${prcconverter}"/>
  </classpath>
  <arg line="-jad ${palmresources}\SOAPClient.jad
            -type Data -o ${palmdeploy}\SOAPClient.prc
            ${palmverified}\SOAPClient.jar"/>
  </java>
</target>
```

This task uses the `MakeMIDPApp` application from MIDP for Palm, located in the `Converter.jar` JAR file. The other command line options for `MakeMIDPApp` are:

```
Usage: java com.sun.midp.palm.database.MakeMIDPApp [-options] <JAR file>
```

where options include:

```
-v                   Verbose output (-v -v gives even more information)
-verbose             Same as -v
-icon <file>         File containing icon for application. Must be in
                     bmp, pbm, or bin (Palm Resource) format.
-smallicon <file>    Same as -smallicon
-name <name>         Short name of application, seen in the launcher
-longname <name>     Long name for the application, seen in beaming, etc.
-creator <crid>      Creator ID for the application
-type <type>         File type for application (default is appl)
-outfile <outfile>   Name of file to create on local disk; this is the
                     file that is downloaded to the Palm
-o <outfile>         Same as -outfile
-version <string>    Change version
```

```
-help                  Print this message
-jad <file>            Specify a file for JAD, MIDlet Suite Packaging
```

Palm recommends that Palm developers use a unique Creator ID for their applications. Creator IDs are a four-character identifier and can be registered on the Palm developer Web site at `http://dev.palmos.com/creatorid/`.

Once registered, developers can set the Creator ID for their applications using the `-creator` option. If this option is not specified, a unique identifier will be created automatically.

The PRC file resulting from this step is put into the `${palmdeploy}` directory, and it can be copied to the Palm using the Install tool in Palm Desktop.

If we want to run the Palm application on the emulator, there are two choices. First, we can use the Wireless Toolkit's emulator script, which is how the Ant build target `SOAPClient` works:

```
<target name="SOAPClient" depends="SOAPClientJAR">
  <exec dir=".\" executable="${wtk-base}\bin\emulatorw.exe">
    <arg line="-Xdevice:PalmOS_Device
               -Xdescriptor:${palmresources}\SOAPClient.jad
               -Xprefs:${palmresources}\emulator-prefs.txt"/>
  </exec>
</target>
```

This target does not use the PRC file, but rather uses the JAD we created previously. The benefit of using this method is that the emulator starts and runs the application automatically.

The other option is to start the emulator and load the PRC manually. To load the PRC, start the emulator and right-click on the screen. Select "Install Application/Database" and navigate to the directory in which the PRC is located. This will load the PRC into the Unfiled category (unless you have loaded the application previously and moved it elsewhere). Find the icon and tap on it to run the application.

Running Java Applications on the PocketPC

This book uses PersonalJava 1.2 for developing Java applications on the PocketPC. Since the Jeode JVM[2] is an implementation of PersonalJava 1.2, we must use a Java 1.1 compiler to compile source code for running on the

---

2. The Jeode JVM is distributed on the application CD accompanying iPaqs and many other PocketPCs. It may not be installed out-of-the-box, but it is simple to install from the CD. Alternatively, Jeode can be purchased from `http://www.handango.com`.

PocketPC. The Ant build target `CompilePocketPC` compiles the PocketPC source code.

```
<target name="CompilePocketPC" depends="CompileDesktop">
  <!-- Compile the PocketPC source code -->
  <javac srcdir="${pocketpcsource}"
    target="1.1"
    bootclasspath="${jdk-base}\lib\classes.zip"
    destdir="${pocketpcdestination}"
    fork="true"
    executable="${jdk-base}\bin\javac"
    compiler="javac1.1">
    <classpath>
      <pathelement location="${desktoplib}\javaonpdas-desktop.jar"/>
      <pathelement location="${pocketpclib}\${pocketpcsoaplib}"/>
    </classpath>
  </javac>
  <jar jarfile="${pocketpcdestination}\pocketpc.jar"
      basedir="${pocketpcdestination}"
      includes="**\*.class"
  />
</target>
```

This build target compiles the source code with the Java 1.1 compiler, and produces a JAR called `pocketpc.jar`.

The `DeployPocketPC` build target copies the `pocketpc.jar` file to the `${pocketpcdeploy}` directory, which is set to `PocketPC My Documents\Java-OnPDAs` on the PC. Files copied to `PocketPC My Documents` are copied to the PocketPC by ActiveSync.

```
<target name="DeployPocketPC" depends="CompilePocketPC">
  <copy file="${pocketpcdestination}\pocketpc.jar"
      todir="${pocketpcdeploy}" />
  <copy todir="${pocketpcdeploy}">
    <fileset dir="${pocketpclib}"/>
  </copy>
</target>
```

Once the JAR file is copied to the PocketPC, we need to create a shortcut to start the Jeode JVM (`evm.exe`) and run the application. A shortcut file is a text file that looks like this:

```
18#"\Windows\evm.exe" <command line options> <class name>
```

For example, to run the application `BasicWindow` (discussed in a subsequent chapter), we need a shortcut file as follows:

```
18#"\Windows\evm.exe" -Xnowinceconsole ↵
-cp "\My Documents\JavaOnPDAs\pocketpc.jar" ↵
com.javaonpdas.ui.BasicWindow
```

The -Xnowinceconsole option indicates to Jeode to not start a Java console. A console would be useful for applications that use System.out.println as a debugging tool. In this case, the option would be -Xwinceconsole.

Another useful Jeode command line option is -Djeode.evm.console.local.keep=TRUE, which tells Jeode to keep the console open after the application has stopped. For other Jeode command line options, refer to Appendix C, "Jeode -D Properties," on page 215 and Appendix D, "Jeode -X Options," on page 221.

To create a shortcut file, the Ant build file includes a CreateShortCuts target, which creates a shortcut for each application in the book.

As an example, the following line from the CreateShortCuts target creates the BasicWindow shortcut described above:

```
<echo message="18#&quot;\Windows\evm.exe&quot; -Xnowinceconsole -cp
&quot;\My Documents\JavaOnPDAs\pocketpc.jar&quot;
com.javaonpdas.ui.BasicWindow"
      file="${pocketpcshortcuts}\BasicWindow.lnk"/>
```

This creates the shortcut file on the PC, but it is not yet on the PocketPC. Files with .lnk extensions cannot be copied to the PocketPC through the PocketPC My Documents directory as we did with the JAR file, so we need to copy the shortcuts to the JavaOnPDAs directory in Mobile Device directly. This is done in Windows Explorer by opening the tree under Mobile Device and copying the .lnk file to the JavaOnPDAs folder. Figure 3.5 shows an example view of the folder structure under Mobile Device.

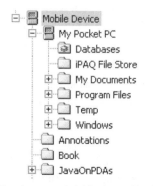

Figure 3.5   The Mobile Device tree in Windows Explorer

The application can then be started on the PocketPC by tapping on the shortcut.

Summary

In this chapter we have prepared a development environment for developing PDA applications in Java. The tool set used in the book and set up in this chapter is entirely free, which is good news if you are a Java developer learning to create applications for PDAs on a budget.

In the subsequent chapters we will make use of this environment to explore the functionality available to the Java developer on Palm devices and the PocketPC.

CHAPTER 4

Things to Think About When Designing for Small Devices

Although the Palm IIIx has about the same computational power, and about four times as much memory, as the first Apple Mac, it is considered a "constrained" device. In comparison to the vast resources of the average desktop computer, the Palm device is an example of a constrained device because its resources are far less than the devices we may normally target with our desktop applications. The standard approaches to software design may not apply for Palm device applications.

Although this chapter focusses on Palm devices, the considerations are relevant to any constrained device. PocketPC devices are less constrained than typical Palm devices in terms of memory, but many of the design considerations for small devices still apply.

As desktop computers have become more and more powerful, software is doing far more work than before. The resources of the hardware on which these applications run is practically unlimited. This power has enabled more elegant software designs, which allow applications to be maintained more easily and to support change as requirements change. Such change may mean changing large parts of the application. Software design techniques have developed ways to isolate change in an application. Isolated change means that other parts of the application are not affected; this, in turn, means that components supporting existing functionality do not need to be touched.

This helps the application's design support change in a more predictable and orderly fashion, often despite the unpredictable nature of future changes.

In a portable device, however, these design principles may not always suit the more constrained environment. On a portable device, the design priorities change. Limited resources must be allocated to features to gain their maximum effect. Speed of execution, use of memory, and screen space become more important than an elegant design that may be pure from an object-oriented perspective and allows changes to be isolated.

This chapter discusses the software design issues that arise when the target is a constrained device. These issues are related to the amount of CPU power in the device, the size of the screen, and the amount of memory available.

Design Issue 1—Constrained Computational Capability

A desktop PC is powered by an unlimited supply of electricity, and so can afford to run at high speed and dissipate large amounts of heat. A Palm device, on the other hand, is a portable device with electricity supplied by two AAA 1.5 V batteries. The designers of the Palm device chose a relatively low-powered CPU to run the Palm in order to conserve battery life and therefore to reduce the frequency with which the batteries needed to be replaced or recharged. Although this was the right decision for a small portable device, it means that software written for the Palm must be developed with a keen eye toward the amount of processing the CPU is being asked to perform.

The other important factor is that tasks performed on PDAs must be done very quickly. The PDA user wants to perform simple tasks that are completed fairly quickly; the user does not want to wait for the device to finish lengthy computation tasks. Palm applications are (and must be) very responsive—at least as responsive as a desktop PC performing an average task. If we agreed that a desktop PC is at least 10 times more powerful than a PDA, then to maintain the same level of responsiveness, the PDA application needs to limit itself to tasks that are 10 times simpler.

Inasmuch as we are using the same language that we have used on desktop applications with great effect, it is tempting to just develop applications in the same way. In our desktop applications we have taken advantage of the cheap power of modern PCs and employed vast and rich class libraries to produce simple and elegant applications. We have used XML parsers for reading configuration files and for detokenizing messages passed as XML documents; motivated by the value of a human-readable message format, we are unbothered by the negligible power taken by our desktop application to do so.

In developing applications in Java on PDAs, it is important to remember that the desktop approach to software design cannot be applied without consideration of the platform differences, and in particular the availability of resources. A design goal for any application on PDAs is to off-load as much work as possible to another computer, which may be the desktop or server.

Design Issue 2—Constrained Screen Size

Designing for simplicity and ease of use is a consistently important aspect of design, regardless of the technology or the medium. A screen with a large number of controls or displayed information takes more time for the user to absorb what is being displayed. Such applications are more "fiddly" than those in which controls and displayed information is displayed sparingly on a screen. Increasing the number of buttons on a screen increases the time it takes to learn an application.[1]

In MIDP on the Palm, the Form is not limited to a particular size when appending Items. For example, if you wanted to add 20 StringItems to a Form, there is nothing to stop you from doing it. In Figure 4.1, the MIDlet has 20 StringItems on the Form, but only 11 are visible without scrolling down. Tapping on the down arrow shows the remainder.

Even though it is possible to add more Items than can be seen on the Form, it is not recommended. An application is made a bit more approachable if scrolling screens are avoided. To avoid the screen in our example, use a list to display the information.

Design Issue 3—Constrained Memory Size

When we say that the Palm is a constrained memory environment, what does that mean to an application developer? First of all, let's have a look at how memory is organized in Palm OS.

Memory Organization

To understand memory organization on MIDP on Palm OS, start a MIDP application. Select the Options menu and then select Memory Info. A dialog similar to that of Figure 4.2 will appear.

---

1. For more guidelines for how to design a Palm application that is easy to use and consistent with other Palm applications, refer to "Palm OS Programmer's Companion," Document Number 3004-003. This document is part of the Palm OS Software Development Kit.

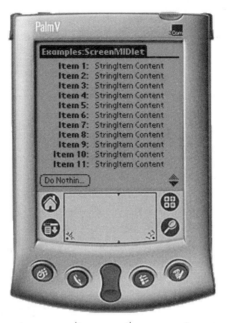

Figure 4.1   There are too many items on the screen to see without scrolling

Figure 4.2   A dialog showing memory information

The types of memory displayed in Figure 4.2 are explained in Table 4.1. Note that these descriptions are specific to the KVM and Sun's implementation of MIDP for Palm OS.

Table 4.1 Types of Memory

Type	Description
rom	The size of the ROM image on this device.
ram	The combined size of RAM on this device. Palm OS divides RAM into two logical areas: dynamic and storage. Both areas remain intact when the device is switched off, but a reset will clear out the dynamic area.
freeram	The combined size of available storage heap and dynamic memory heap on this device.
	"Dynamic heap" refers to the area of RAM implemented as a single heap that is used for dynamic allocations such as application stacks, application dynamic allocations, and system dynamic allocations. In a Palm OS 3.5 device with 4 MB or more, the dynamic heap space is 256 KB. This amount of memory is set aside whether or not it is currently used for dynamic allocations.
	"Storage heap" refers to the remainder of RAM. There can be one or more storage heaps. Storage heaps are used to store nonvolatile data, such as databases.
	In all versions of Palm OS to date, the maximum chunk of storage RAM that can be obtained by an application is slightly less than 64 KB.[a]
freeheap	The size of the available memory in the storage heap.
maxheapchunk	The size of the largest chunk in the dynamic heap.
javafreeheap	The amount of memory available in the Java heap. The Java heap is the area of the dynamic heap that is used by Java when allocating new objects as well as objects on the application's stack. As it is a chunk of memory from the dynamic heap, its maximum value is slightly less than 64 KB.
permanent	The amount of memory allocated internally by the KVM.

a. The 64 KB limit is increased in Palm OS 5.0.

Memory Usage

To see how much memory is available to the developer, we can write a simple application. There are two methods in the `Runtime` class that are useful for working out available memory. They are `totalMemory` and `freeMemory`. The following code fragment shows how to determine the memory available inside a MIDlet:

```
Runtime runtime = Runtime.getRuntime();
runtime.gc();
System.out.println("Total: " + runtime.totalMemory() +
  " Free: " + runtime.freeMemory());
```

Note that we use the `Runtime` method `gc` before calling the `freeMemory` method. The purpose of this call is to prompt the virtual machine to clean up unused objects that may not have been garbage collected because the amount of memory is not sufficiently low to trigger a routine garbage collection.

The amount of memory returned by `freeMemory` can be different from the amount of memory reported by `javafreeheap` in the `Options | Memory Info` dialog. This is because `javafreeheap` refers to the internal Java dynamic heap used for stack and new Java objects, while `freeMemory` returns an approximation of the amount of memory available for future allocated objects.

The MIDlets `MemoryMIDlet`, `StaticMemoryMIDlet`, and `MultipleClassMIDlet` each perform a different memory allocation. `MemoryMIDlet` allocates a new array of 1000 bytes.

```
Runtime runtime = Runtime.getRuntime();
runtime.gc();
beforeFree = runtime.freeMemory();
largeArray = new byte[1000];
runtime.gc();
afterFree = runtime.freeMemory();
System.out.println("Total: " + runtime.totalMemory() +
  " Free (before): " + beforeFree +
  " Free (after): " + afterFree);
```

`StaticMemoryMIDlet` does the same thing, but also has a static array of 2000 bytes:

```
static byte[] largeStaticArray = new byte[2000];
```

Finally, `MultipleClassMIDlet` creates an instance of `LargeClass`, a class that has an attribute that references an array of 1000 bytes:

```
LargeClass largeClass = new LargeClass();
```

where `LargeClass` is defined as:

```
package com.javaonpdas.small;

public class LargeClass {

  private byte[] byteArray = new byte[1000];

  public String method1(String s1, String s2) {
    return s1+s2;
  }

  public String method2(String s1, String s2) {
    return s1+s2;
  }
}
```

The number of bytes returned by the `freeMemory()` method were recorded before and after the dynamic allocation, and are collated in Table 4.2.

From the table, note that a static array object takes up space from the same Java heap that is used to allocate dynamic objects. That is, statically and dynamically allocated objects use the same heap space. As noted previously, the heap space is restricted to 64 KB in Palm OS 3.X and 4.X.

Table 4.2 Memory Consumed by Static and Dynamic Allocations

MIDlet	Bytes Consumed by Loading the MIDlet	Bytes Further Consumed by Processing the "Allocate" Command	Allocation Performed
MemoryMIDlet	4396	1016	Allocate an array of 1000 bytes
StaticMemoryMIDlet	6412	1016	Allocate an array of 1000 bytes
MultipleClassMIDlet	4392	1032	Allocate a new instance of LargeClass

Summary

In this chapter we have looked at considerations that must be made when targeting resource-constrained devices such as the Palm. It is important to remember that each static and dynamic allocation of memory—such as creating a new object—consumes a very limited resource. In addition, screen space for a small hand-held device is limited. To ensure the usability of the application, it is important to increase responsiveness and reduce the amount of information on the screen. In addition to memory and screen size considerations, the limited processing power of PDAs emphasizes the goal in a distributed application design of doing as much of the work on the server as possible.

CHAPTER 5

The User Interface

The user interface is a part of any application that is well worth spending a lot of time on, as it is the only part of the application that the user sees. A user tends to (quite rightly) judge the quality of an application on the basis of the elegance and aesthetics of its user interface. In this chapter, we will look at how best to use the user interface classes available in the MID profile and PersonalJava to develop a user interface on a PDA.

User Interfaces in MIDP

The user interface classes of the MID profile are found in the lcdui package (javax.microedition.lcdui). The class diagram in Figure 5.1 shows most of the classes in the package.

In the following sections, we will have a look at the main classes that we will use to create a user interface for our Palm OS applications.

Displayable

Displayable is the parent class of Screen and Canvas, which provide the foundations of each application's user interface. A Displayable can have a number of Commands, which are visual objects used to initiate some action in the application. A Command can be implemented in a variety of ways, including as

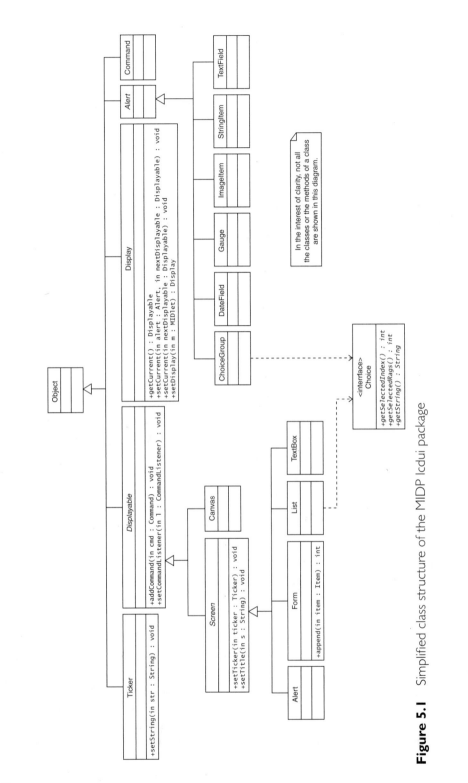

Figure 5.1 Simplified class structure of the MIDP lcdui package

In the interest of clarity, not all the classes or the methods of a class are shown in this diagram.

a button or menu item. A Command has a label, a type, and a priority. The label is a string used to distinguish the Command on the user interface. The command type provides the MIDP implementation a hint as to how to treat this command. Command types are BACK, CANCEL, EXIT, HELP, ITEM, OK, SCREEN, and STOP. By giving a command a CANCEL type, for example, the developer can let the MIDP implementation know that the command represents the user indicating that they do not want to accept the information currently presented on the display. Note that for command types other than SCREEN, the MIDP implementation can override the label with a more appropriate label for the device.

The Command can also be given a priority, which provides another hint to the MIDP implementation, this time with regard to the order with which this command should be displayed in relation to other commands on the same display. A lower number indicates a higher priority.

For example, to create a new command that represents an action to exit the application, we would write the following:

```
Command exitCommand = new Command("Exit", Command.EXIT, 10);
```

As an application style, we have indicated that the exit button should appear last in the display's commands, and so we have assigned it a lower priority.

Once an application has created its command objects, an object that implements the interface CommandListener is assigned to listen for them to be activated. This is done with the setCommandListener method, invoked on an object whose class is a subclass of Displayable. The CommandListener interface specifies one method, commandAction, which is passed the Command being activated, and the Displayable object to which it belongs.

The difference between a Screen and a Canvas is that a Screen is used as the basis for building a typical form-based user interface, while a Canvas is used for drawing images, lines, and circles. In this chapter, we will mainly focus on user interfaces built with Screens.

There are four types of Screen: Alert, Form, List, and TextBox. Any one of them can have added Command objects, as well as be given a title. In the following code examples, we will use a Form to start off each example, so let's have a look at the Form first.

Form

A Form is a special type of Screen, in that it can accept Items. An Item is a simple user interface control, several of which can appear on the one Form. Subclasses of Item are multiple- or single-selection buttons, date and time selection controls, a gauge to show a value in a range, an image control, a string control, and a text entry control.

To create an empty form:

```
Form mainForm = new Form("BaseUIMIDlet");
```

Then, to create an exit command so that we can exit our MIDlet:

```
Command exitCommand = new Command("Exit", Command.EXIT, 10);
```

Because an application can have many `Displayable` objects (that is, many instances of Forms, Alerts, Lists, TextBoxes, and Canvases), and because only one `Displayable` can occupy the device's display at one time, we need a way to specify which `Displayable` should be visible. This is done with the `Display` class. With a `Display` object, we can find out which `Displayable` is currently visible, and we can set a `Displayable` to become visible. Each MIDlet has one `Display`. To obtain a reference to it, we use the static method `getDisplay` on the `Display` class, passing it a reference to the `MIDlet` object.

So, for our example, we'll need a `Display` object reference:

```
Display display = null;
```

In the MIDlet's constructor, we add the exit command and set the MIDlet to be the command listener:

```
mainForm.addCommand(exitCommand);
mainForm.setCommandListener(this);
```

In the `startApp` method, we obtain a reference to the MIDlet's display, and set the current display to our newly created form:

```
display = Display.getDisplay(this);
display.setCurrent(mainForm);
```

Because we have set the MIDlet to be the command listener for our exit command, we need to implement the `commandAction` method and to take some appropriate action when the exit command event occurs. For our simple example:

```
public void commandAction(Command c, Displayable d) {
  if (c == exitCommand) {
    destroyApp(false);
    notifyDestroyed();
  }
}
```

The following code shows how we put all this together. Because we would like all our examples to have the same basic behavior, the `BaseUIMIDlet` class will also provide the base class for all our user interface examples.

```
package com.javaonpdas.ui;

import javax.microedition.midlet.*;
import javax.microedition.lcdui.*;

public class BaseUIMIDlet extends MIDlet
  implements CommandListener {

  protected Form mainForm = new Form("BaseUIMIDlet");
  protected Command exitCommand = new Command("Exit",
    Command.EXIT, 10);
  protected Display display = null;
  protected static final String[] MOVIES = {"Gladiator",
                                            "The Patriot",
                                            "A Few Good Men"};
  protected Command okCommand = new Command("OK",
    Command.SCREEN, 1);
  protected Command backCommand = new Command("Back",
    Command.SCREEN, 2);

  public BaseUIMIDlet() {
    mainForm.addCommand(exitCommand);
    mainForm.setCommandListener(this);
  }

  public void startApp() {
    display = Display.getDisplay(this);
    display.setCurrent(mainForm);
  }

  public void pauseApp() {
  }

  public void destroyApp(boolean unconditional) {
  }

  public void commandAction(Command c, Displayable d) {
    if (c == exitCommand) {
      destroyApp(false);
      notifyDestroyed();
    }
  }
}
```

Figure 5.2   The startup screen of BaseUIMIDlet

Figure 5.2 shows how the Form looks after starting up.

In this example, as shown in Figure 5.3, the exit command has been implemented not as a button on the screen, but as a menu item under the Go menu.

If we had specified the command type of the exit command to be SCREEN, it would have appeared as an exit button on the screen, as in Figure 5.4.

Although the MIDP implementation can override the label of a command, the Palm OS implementation tends not to do so. If we specified that the label of the exit command should be "Boo!" the label remains "Boo!". If we change the command type to HELP, the label remains "Boo!", but it is moved to the Options menu, as shown in Figure 5.5.

As we discovered previously, the MIDP implementation determines how Command objects are rendered, according to the device's capabilities. On a Palm device using MIDP for Palm, Command objects with type SCREEN are rendered as buttons along the bottom of the screen. If there are too many Commands, or their labels make the buttons too large to fit along the bottom of the screen, the remaining Commands are rendered as menu items on the Actions menu.

In the following example, we will create six Commands, all of command type SCREEN, with equal priority, and add them to the form. Note that we are

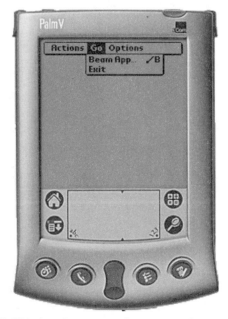

Figure 5.3 BaseUIMIDlet's exit command as a menu item

Figure 5.4 BaseUIMIDlet's exit command as a button on the screen

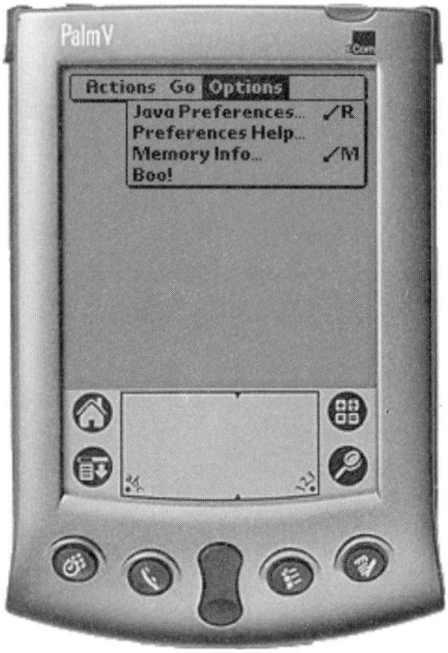

Figure 5.5　Changing the type to Command.HELP

subclassing `BaseUIMIDlet`, as we will do for all our examples, so that we get the same fundamental behavior (and save some retyping work).

```
package com.javaonpdas.ui;

import javax.microedition.lcdui.*;

public class CommandMIDlet extends BaseUIMIDlet {

  private Command command1Command =
    new Command("1", Command.SCREEN, 1);
  private Command command2Command =
    new Command("2", Command.SCREEN, 1);
  private Command command3Command =
    new Command("3", Command.SCREEN, 1);
  private Command command4Command =
    new Command("4", Command.SCREEN, 1);
  private Command command5Command =
    new Command("5", Command.SCREEN, 1);
  private Command command6Command =
    new Command("6", Command.SCREEN, 1);
```

```
public CommandMIDlet() {
  super();
  mainForm.setTitle("CommandMIDlet");
  mainForm.addCommand(command1Command);
  mainForm.addCommand(command2Command);
  mainForm.addCommand(command3Command);
  mainForm.addCommand(command4Command);
  mainForm.addCommand(command5Command);
  mainForm.addCommand(command6Command);
  }
}
```

Figure 5.6 shows how the Commands have been rendered. Note that although the labels are quite short, only five of the six commands have been rendered on the screen as buttons.

To see the full set of six commands, we need to go to the Actions menu, as seen in Figure 5.7.

Another type of Screen is the Alert. Because we will use Alerts to display information in subsequent sections, let's have a look at Alerts now.

Figure 5.6 Rendering commands

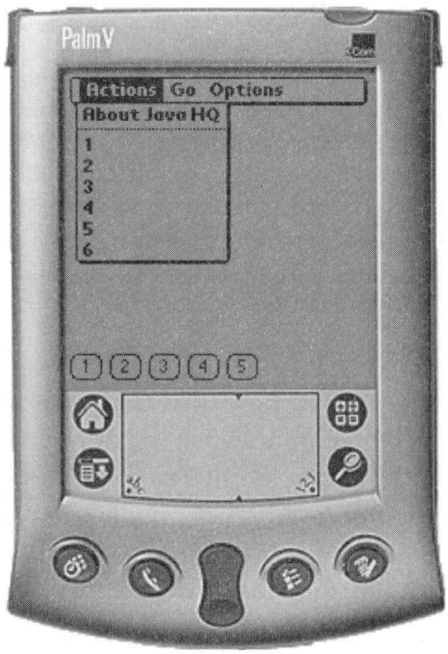

Figure 5.7   The full set of commands

Alert

An Alert is a screen that displays text and optionally an image. Typically, an Alert is used to display some information for the user or to indicate that some urgent action needs to be taken. An Alert can time out automatically, or be displayed until the user acknowledges it.

To create an alert and set its time-out (to five seconds, for example), the following code is used:

```
Alert alert = new Alert("Alert");
alert.setTimeout(5000);
alert.setString("This is an alert that is displayed for 5 seconds");
```

To display the alert, and go back to the main form when the alert times out, we can use the setCurrent method that takes an Alert and Displayable as parameters.

```
display.setCurrent(alert, mainForm);
```

This simple alert is rendered on a Palm device as shown in Figure 5.8.

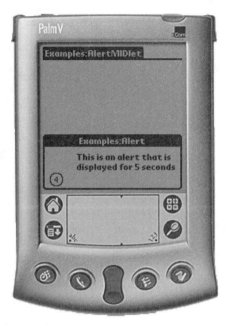

Figure 5.8 Rendering an alert

The numbers displayed in the circle in the lower left corner of the Alert indicate the number of seconds remaining until the Alert will time-out.

There are two ways that the alert will not be automatically acknowledged. The first is if the alert's string is too large to display on the screen. In this case, regardless of the alert's time-out value, the alert will stay on the screen until the user acknowledges it.

Such an alert is shown in Figure 5.9.

Note that the alert's time-out value is ignored.

There is another way to display the alert so that it is manually acknowledged, using the time-out value FOREVER, as in the following code fragment:

```
Alert alert = new Alert("Alert");
alert.setTimeout(Alert.FOREVER);
alert.setString("This is a short string");
display.setCurrent(alert, mainForm);
```

For this alert, the MIDP implementation renders a Done button, as shown in Figure 5.10.

An Alert can also have an alert type, which indicates the nature of the alert. The choices are CONFIRMATION (Figure 5.11), WARNING (Figure 5.12),

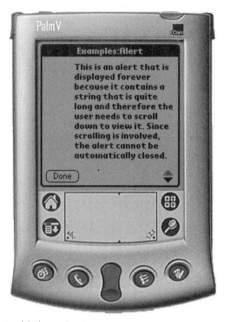

Figure 5.9   An alert with long text

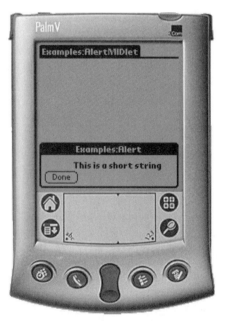

Figure 5.10   An alert with short text

INFO (Figure 5.13), ERROR (Figure 5.14), and ALARM (Figure 5.15). The alert type effects the icon displayed in the Alert. The screen portion shots in Figures 5.11 through 5.15 show how these are rendered on a Palm device.

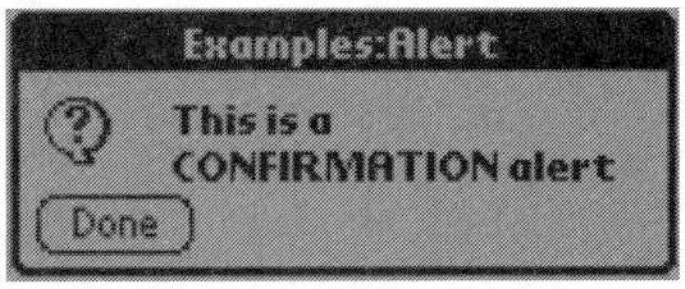

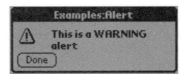

Figure 5.11   A confirmation alert

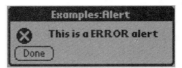

Figure 5.12   A warning alert

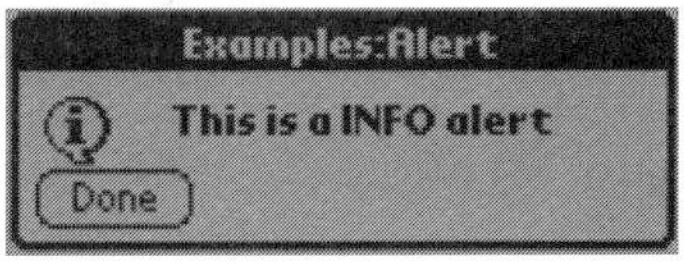

Figure 5.13   An information alert

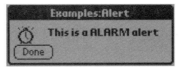

Figure 5.14   An error alert

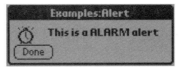

Figure 5.15   An alarm alert

The AlertType can also be used to play a sound to accompany the alert. The sound is limited to the capabilities of the device. To play the WARNING sound:

```
AlertType.WARNING.playSound(display);
```

An Alert is a useful way to display a small amount of information to the user, and we will use them in the following examples to build on our knowledge of Forms.

To create more sophisticated user interfaces, we have the ability to add objects of class Item to the Form. In the following sections, we will look at each Item available. Note that Items can only appear on Forms.

ChoiceGroup

A ChoiceGroup is used for obtaining a single selection or multiple selections from a group of choices. The MIDP implementation determines how the choice group is rendered. On a Palm device, single selection choice groups are rendered as drop down lists, while multiple selection choice groups are rendered as check boxes.

A single selection choice group is created like this:

```
protected static final String[] MEDIA = {"DVD", "VHS"};
protected Command choiceCommand =
    new Command("Choice", Command.SCREEN, 1);
```

For this example, we have chosen the constructor that allows the choice labels to be specified as an array of strings. We have chosen to not specify images to accompany the choices, indicated by setting the last parameter of the constructor to null. Note that there is also the IMPLICIT choice type. The only difference between EXCLUSIVE and IMPLICIT is that it is possible to register a CommandListener object for the IMPLICIT type, and the CommandListener is notified whenever the selection changes. There is no notification for the EXCLUSIVE type.

Then we can add the choice group to a form:

```
Form choiceForm = new Form("Movie Selection");
choiceForm.append(singleChoice);
```

In the command listener for the form and to obtain the selection when the user indicates that they are finished use the following:

```
int i = singleChoice.getSelectedIndex();
String mediaSelected = singleChoice.getString(i);
```

For choices where multiple selections are valid, the MULTIPLE choice group type is used:

```
ChoiceGroup multipleChoice =
  new ChoiceGroup("Movies", ChoiceGroup.MULTIPLE, MOVIES, null);
```

To obtain the selections, an array of Boolean flags is used by the getSelectedFlags method:

```
boolean[] selections = new boolean[multipleChoice.size()];
multipleChoice.getSelectedFlags(selections);
```

The Boolean flag corresponding to the choice is set to true if the user selected that choice. For example, to build up a string of the user's selections, we could use the following code fragment:

```
String movieSelected = new String();
boolean[] selections = new boolean[multipleChoice.size()];
multipleChoice.getSelectedFlags(selections);
for (int j=0; j<selections.length; j++)
  if (selections[j])
    movieSelected += multipleChoice.getString(j) +
      " on " + mediaSelected + "\n";
```

Putting all this together, the MIDlet ChoiceGroupMIDlet displays a form with a single selection choice group and a multiple selection choice group. When the user presses the OK button, an alert is displayed with the user's selections from the two groups.

```
package com.javaonpdas.ui;

import javax.microedition.lcdui.*;

public class ChoiceGroupMIDlet extends BaseUIMIDlet {

  protected static final String[] MEDIA = {"DVD", "VHS"};
  protected Command choiceCommand =
    new Command("Choice", Command.SCREEN, 1);

  public ChoiceGroupMIDlet() {
    super();
    mainForm.setTitle("ChoiceGroupMIDlet");
    mainForm.addCommand(choiceCommand);
  }
```

```
    public void commandAction(Command c, Displayable d) {
      if (c == choiceCommand) {
        Form choiceForm = new Form("Movie Selection");
        ChoiceGroup singleChoice = new ChoiceGroup("Media",
          ChoiceGroup.EXCLUSIVE, MEDIA, null);
        ChoiceGroup multipleChoice = new ChoiceGroup("Movies",
          ChoiceGroup.MULTIPLE, MOVIES, null);
        choiceForm.append(singleChoice);
        choiceForm.append(multipleChoice);
        choiceForm.addCommand(okCommand);
        choiceForm.addCommand(backCommand);
        choiceForm.addCommand(exitCommand);
        choiceForm.setCommandListener(this);
        display.setCurrent(choiceForm);
      }
      else if (c == okCommand) {
        Form choiceForm = (Form)d;
        ChoiceGroup singleChoice =
          (ChoiceGroup)(choiceForm.get(0));
        ChoiceGroup multipleChoice =
          (ChoiceGroup)(choiceForm.get(1));
        // get the media selection
        int i = singleChoice.getSelectedIndex();
        String mediaSelected = singleChoice.getString(i);
        // get the movie selection
        String movieSelected = new String();
        boolean[] selections = new boolean[multipleChoice.size()];
        multipleChoice.getSelectedFlags(selections);
        for (int j=0; j<selections.length; j++)
          if (selections[j])
            movieSelected += multipleChoice.getString(j) +
            " on " + mediaSelected + "\n";
        // display the result
        Alert alert = new Alert("Selection");
        alert.setString(movieSelected);
        alert.setTimeout(5000);
        alert.setType(AlertType.INFO);
        display.setCurrent(alert, mainForm);
      }
      else if (c == backCommand) {
        display.setCurrent(mainForm);
      }
      else {
        super.commandAction(c, d);
      }
    }
  }
```

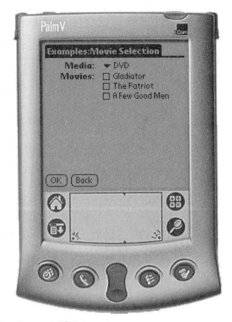

Figure 5.16   ChoiceGroupMIDlet

The choice group form is shown in Figure 5.16.

When the OK button is pressed, the MIDlet displays the alert with the selections (Figure 5.17).

DateField

The DateField class provides a way for dates and times to be displayed and entered. The following code fragment shows how to display a DateField.

```
DateField startDateField =
  new DateField("Loan Date", DateField.DATE_TIME);
startDateField.setDate(new Date());
mainForm.append(startDateField);
```

The date and time displayed on the field is set with a Date object. In the example above, the current date and time is used. If we wanted to set the date field to, for example, tomorrow night at 10:00 P.M., we could do the following:

```
DateField returnDateField =
  new DateField("Return Date", DateField.DATE_TIME);
Calendar calendar = Calendar.getInstance();
```

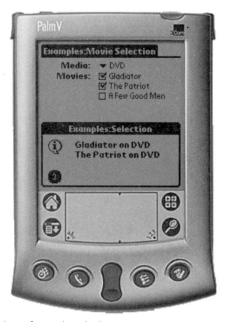

Figure 5.17   Selections from the choice group

```
calendar.setTime(tomorrow());
calendar.set(Calendar.HOUR, 10);
calendar.set(Calendar.MINUTE, 0);
calendar.set(Calendar.AM_PM, Calendar.PM);
returnDateField.setDate(calendar.getTime());
mainForm.append(returnDateField);
```

Because we don't have date calculations in MIDP, we need to work out the date for the following day like this:

```
private Date tomorrow() {
  Date today = new Date();
  Date tomorrow = new Date(today.getTime()+(24*60*60*1000));
  return tomorrow;
}
```

Figure 5.18 shows two `DateFields` on a `Form`.

When the date field is selected, a date editing dialog is displayed, as shown in Figure 5.19. Note that the standard Palm OS date editor has been used by the MIDP implementation.

When the `DateField`'s time field is selected, the standard Palm time editor is displayed, as shown in Figure 5.20.

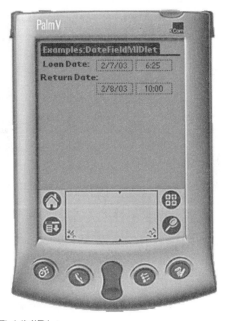

Figure 5.18   DateFieldMIDlet

Figure 5.19   Selecting a date

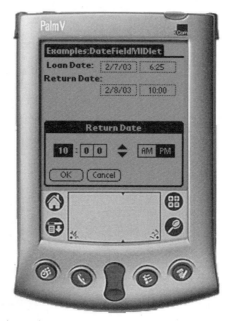

Figure 5.20   Selecting a time

Gauge

The Gauge class is used to display (and optionally edit) a value within a range. The following code fragment shows how to create and display a gauge:

```
Gauge gauge = new Gauge("Value", true, 20, 5);
gaugeForm.append(gauge);
```

The first parameter of the Gauge constructor specifies the gauge's label. The second is a Boolean to indicate whether the gauge should be editable. The third parameter is the maximum value of the range of values for the gauge, whereas the last parameter is the initial value.

Figure 5.21 shows how the gauge looks on the Palm device.

Clicking on the arrows at each end of the field will increase or decrease the value.

To retrieve the value set by the user, we use the getValue method on the gauge object.

If the gauge is not editable (for example, if the flag was set to false in the constructor), the gauge is rendered like a bar graph, as Figure 5.22 shows.

Figure 5.21   GaugeMIDlet

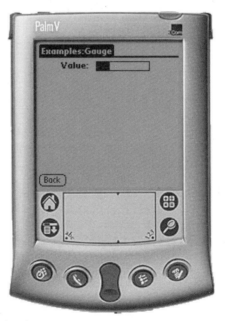

Figure 5.22   A read-only gauge

StringItem

A `StringItem` is an `Item` for displaying static text on a `Form`. It consists of a label and the text itself. The text of a `StringItem` cannot be edited by the user.

The following code fragment shows how to create a `StringItem` and add it to a `Form`:

```
StringItem addressLine1 =
  new StringItem("Address Line 1", "10 Main Street");
stringItemForm.append(addressLine1);
```

The following code shows how a `StringItem` could be used in an application:

```
package com.javaonpdas.ui;

import javax.microedition.lcdui.*;

public class StringItemMIDlet extends BaseUIMIDlet {

  private Command stringItemCommand =
    new Command("StringItem", Command.SCREEN, 1);

  public StringItemMIDlet() {
    super();
    mainForm.setTitle("StringItemMIDlet");
    mainForm.addCommand(stringItemCommand);
  }

  public void commandAction(Command c, Displayable d) {
    if (c == stringItemCommand) {
      Form stringItemForm = new Form("Your address details");
      StringItem addressLine1 =
        new StringItem("Address Line 1", "10 Main Street");
      StringItem addressLine2 =
        new StringItem("Address Line 2", "Townsville");
      StringItem postcode = new StringItem("Postcode", "7423");
      stringItemForm.append(addressLine1);
      stringItemForm.append(addressLine2);
      stringItemForm.append(postcode);
      stringItemForm.addCommand(backCommand);
      stringItemForm.addCommand(exitCommand);
      stringItemForm.setCommandListener(this);
      display.setCurrent(stringItemForm);
    }
    else if (c == backCommand) {
      display.setCurrent(mainForm);
    }
```

```
    else {
      super.commandAction(c, d);
    }
  }
}
```

Figure 5.23 shows how the `StringItemForm` is displayed.

TextField

A `TextField` item is similar in appearance to a `StringItem`, except that a `TextField` is used for allowing the user to modify or enter text. A `TextField` can also filter the text that is entered into the field; the filter is called an input constraint.

To create a `TextField` with the text content initialized, the following constructor is used:

```
TextField addressLine1 =
  new TextField("Address Line 1", "10 Main Street",
                20, TextField.ANY);
```

The last parameter of the constructor is where the input constraints can be specified. The available constraints are ANY, EMAILADDR, NUMERIC, PASSWORD,

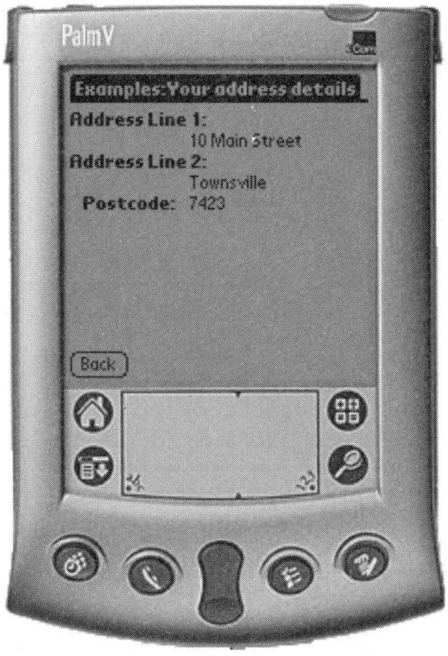

Figure 5.23 StringItemMIDlet

PHONENUMBER, and URL. In each case, only the input indicated by the constraint will be accepted by the field.

When the user has finished modifying or entering the text, the field's text can be retrieved by calling the getString method.

The following code shows how a TextField could be used in an application:

```java
package com.javaonpdas.ui;

import javax.microedition.lcdui.*;

public class TextFieldMIDlet extends BaseUIMIDlet {

  private Command textFieldCommand =
    new Command("TextField", Command.SCREEN, 1);

  public TextFieldMIDlet() {
    super();
    mainForm.setTitle("TextFieldMIDlet");
    mainForm.addCommand(textFieldCommand);
  }

  public void commandAction(Command c, Displayable d) {
    if (c == textFieldCommand) {
      Form textFieldForm = new Form("Confirm your address");
      TextField addressLine1 = new TextField("Address Line 1",
                                             "10 Main Street",
                                             20,
                                             TextField.ANY);
      TextField addressLine2 = new TextField("Address Line 2",
                                             "Townsville",
                                             20,
                                             TextField.ANY);
      TextField postcode = new TextField("Postcode", "7423",
                                         4, TextField.NUMERIC);
      textFieldForm.append(addressLine1);
      textFieldForm.append(addressLine2);
      textFieldForm.append(postcode);
      textFieldForm.addCommand(okCommand);
      textFieldForm.addCommand(backCommand);
      textFieldForm.addCommand(exitCommand);
      textFieldForm.setCommandListener(this);
      display.setCurrent(textFieldForm);
    }
    else if (c == okCommand) {
      Form textFieldForm = (Form)d;
      TextField addressLine1 =
        (TextField)(textFieldForm.get(0));
```

```
    TextField addressLine2 =
      (TextField)(textFieldForm.get(1));
    TextField postcode = (TextField)(textFieldForm.get(2));
    // display the result
    Alert alert = new Alert("Address Entered");
    alert.setString("The address is:\n" +
                    addressLine1.getString() + "\n" +
                    addressLine2.getString() + "\n" +
                    postcode.getString());
    alert.setTimeout(5000);
    alert.setType(AlertType.INFO);
    display.setCurrent(alert, mainForm);
  }
  else if (c == backCommand) {
    display.setCurrent(mainForm);
  }
  else {
    super.commandAction(c, d);
  }
  }
}
}
```

So far we have looked at two types of Screen: the Alert and the Form. Now we will have a look at the other two types: the List and the TextBox.

List

The List is a type of Screen that enables the user to select single or multiple items in a list. It supports the same Choice interface as the ChoiceGroup item we looked at previously. The List supports the same choice types: IMPLICIT, EXCLUSIVE, and MULTIPLE.

The following code fragment shows the creation of a List, again using the MOVIES static array of strings to set up the choices:

```
List list = new List("Movies", List.EXCLUSIVE, MOVIES, null);
```

Just as in the ChoiceGroup, the selection is retrieved from the List using the getSelectedIndex and getString methods:

```
int i = list.getSelectedIndex();
String movieSelected = list.getString(i);
```

Figure 5.24 shows an EXCLUSIVE List.

A MULTIPLE List is created in a similar fashion, and the selections are retrieved in the same way as multiple selections for a ChoiceGroup.

Figure 5.24   An exclusive list

```
List list = new List("Movies", List.MULTIPLE, MOVIES, null);

...

String movieSelected = new String();
boolean[] selections = new boolean[list.size()];
list.getSelectedFlags(selections);
for (int i=0; i<selections.length; i++)
    if (selections[i])
        movieSelected += list.getString(i) + "\n";
```

The MULTIPLE List is rendered as a list of check boxes, as shown in
Figure 5.25.

TextBox

The TextBox is a type of Screen that allows free-form text entry. On a Palm
device, it is rendered as a standard Memo screen. The TextBox uses the same
input constraints concept as the TextField.

To create a TextBox use the following:

```
TextBox textBox = new TextBox("Movies", "", 20, TextField.ANY);
```

Figure 5.25 A multiple selection list

And to retrieve the string entered:

```
String movieSelected = textBox.getString();
```

Figure 5.26 shows a TextBox on a Palm device.

Ticker

One other interesting thing about the Screen subclasses is that they can have a Ticker. A Ticker is like a ticker-tape display, where a string of text is repeatedly scrolled horizontally across the screen.

A Ticker object is created like this:

```
Ticker ticker = new Ticker("Special: Choose 2 movies for $6...");
```

The Ticker is displayed on any Screen object, using the setTicker method. The following MIDlet is the same as the ChoiceGroupMIDlet, except that this one has a Ticker on each Screen in the application. Figure 5.27 shows the Ticker on a main form. Figure 5.28 shows a ticker on the choice form we used previously. Figure 5.29 shows a ticker on an alert.

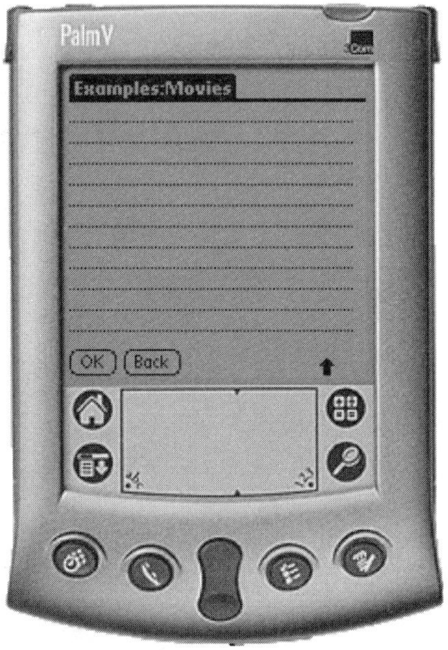

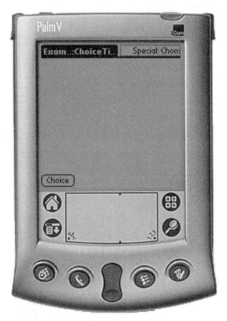

Figure 5.26   TextBoxMIDlet

Figure 5.27   A ticker on the main form

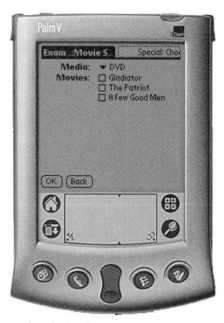

Figure 5.28   Ticker on the choice form

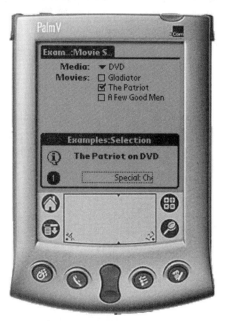

Figure 5.29   Ticker on an alert

User Interfaces in PersonalJava

In PersonalJava, we have available the power of JDK 1.1.8 AWT, except for some differences as noted in Section 5.2 of the PersonalJava 1.2 specification. Rather than include a tutorial on AWT, in this section we will construct some simple user interfaces and show how they appear on the PocketPC.

Frame

A Frame is the enclosing window of an application, and the basis of a simple user interface.

The application below shows a Frame being extended and created:

```
package com.javaonpdas.ui;

import java.awt.*;
import java.awt.event.*;

public class BasicWindow extends Frame {

  public BasicWindow(String title) {
    super(title);
    // handle frame closing events
    addWindowListener(new WindowAdapter() {
      public void windowClosing(WindowEvent e) {
        System.exit(0);
      }
    } );
  }

  public static void main(String[] args) {
    Frame f = new BasicWindow("BasicWindow");
    f.setSize(f.getToolkit().getScreenSize());
    f.show();
  }
}
```

The screen shot in Figure 5.30 shows how this appears on the PocketPC.

Buttons

To add a button to a window, we use the addButton method on the Frame, as follows:

Figure 5.30   BasicWindow

```
Button button1 = new Button("Button 1");
add(button1);
button1.addActionListener(this);
```

Creating three buttons in this way, and using a FlowLayout, we can create
a simple application that writes to the console whenever a button is pressed.

```
package com.javaonpdas.ui;

import java.awt.*;
import java.awt.event.*;

public class Buttons extends Frame implements ActionListener {

  public Buttons(String title) {
    super(title);
    // handle frame closing events
    addWindowListener(new WindowAdapter() {
      public void windowClosing(WindowEvent e) {
        System.exit(0);
      }
    } );
    // add components
    setLayout(new FlowLayout(FlowLayout.LEFT, 10, 10));
    Button button1 = new Button("Button 1");
```

```
   add(button1);
   button1.addActionListener(this);
   Button button2 = new Button("Button 2");
   add(button2);
   button2.addActionListener(this);
   Button button3 = new Button("Button 3");
   add(button3);
   button3.addActionListener(this);
 }

 public void actionPerformed(ActionEvent evt) {
   String cmd = evt.getActionCommand();
   System.out.println(cmd + " was pressed.");
 }

 public static void main(String[] args) {
   Frame f = new Buttons("Buttons");
   f.setSize(f.getToolkit().getScreenSize());
   f.show();
 }
}
```

The screen shot in Figure 5.31 shows how the application looks on the PocketPC.

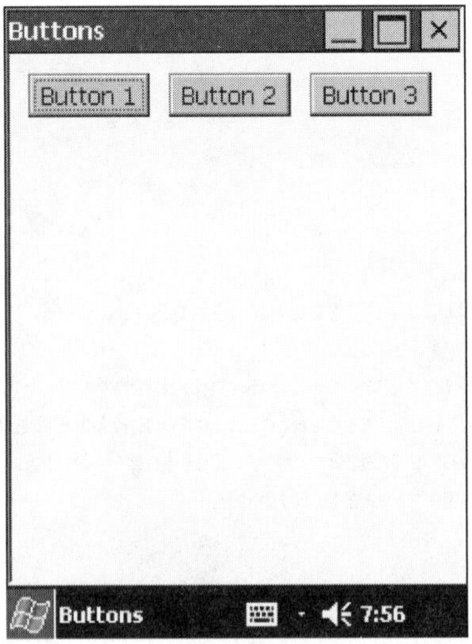

Figure 5.31   Buttons

TextFields

A TextField is used for entering a single line of text. It is created with one of four constructors, as follows:

```
TextField textField1 = new TextField();
TextField textField2 = new TextField("Field 2");
TextField textField3 = new TextField("Field 3",20);
TextField textField4 = new TextField(20);
```

These text fields can be put together into an application, as follows:

```
package com.javaonpdas.ui;

import java.awt.*;
import java.awt.event.*;

public class TextFields extends Frame {

  public TextFields(String title) {
    super(title);
    // handle frame closing events
    addWindowListener(new WindowAdapter() {
      public void windowClosing(WindowEvent e) {
        System.exit(0);
      }
    } );
    // add components
    setLayout(new FlowLayout(FlowLayout.LEFT, 10, 10));
    TextField textField1 = new TextField();
    TextField textField2 = new TextField("Field 2");
    TextField textField3 = new TextField("Field 3",20);
    TextField textField4 = new TextField(20);
    add(textField1);
    add(textField2);
    add(textField3);
    add(textField4);
  }

  public static void main(String[] args) {
    Frame f = new TextFields("TextFields");
    f.setSize(f.getToolkit().getScreenSize());
    f.show();
  }
}
```

Figure 5.32 shows how this appears on the PocketPC.

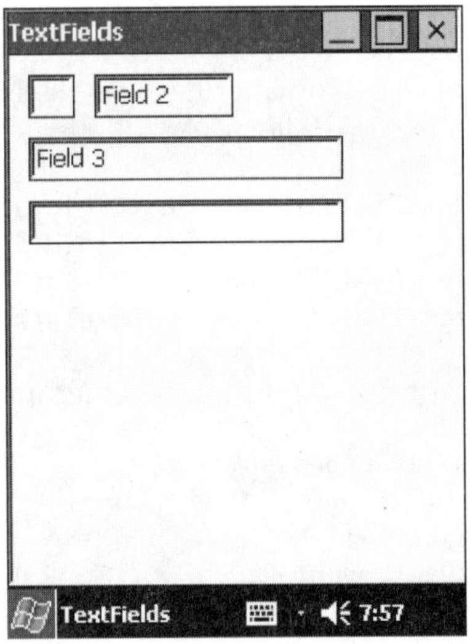

Figure 5.32   TextFields

Lists

Lists are used to display multiple items that can be selected. A List can be set so that a number of items can be displayed without scrolling, regardless of how many items are currently in the list. For example, the following code sets aside enough space for 10 items without scrolling, but it only puts seven items in the list for now:

```
List list = new List(10);
list.add("Item 1");
list.add("Item 2");
list.add("Item 3");
list.add("Item 4");
list.add("Item 5");
list.add("Item 6");
list.add("Item 7");
```

This code can be put into an application as follows:

```
package com.javaonpdas.ui;

import java.awt.*;
import java.awt.event.*;

public class Lists extends Frame {
```

```
public Lists(String title) {
  super(title);
  // handle frame closing events
  addWindowListener(new WindowAdapter() {
    public void windowClosing(WindowEvent e) {
      System.exit(0);
    }
  } );
  // add components
  setLayout(new FlowLayout(FlowLayout.LEFT, 10, 10));
  List list = new List(10);
  list.add("Item 1");
  list.add("Item 2");
  list.add("Item 3");
  list.add("Item 4");
  list.add("Item 5");
  list.add("Item 6");
  list.add("Item 7");
  add(list);
}

public static void main(String[] args) {
  Frame f = new Lists("Lists");
  f.setSize(f.getToolkit().getScreenSize());
  f.show();
}
}
```

Figure 5.33 shows the screen shot.

Checkboxes

Checkboxes are used for making a choice of a small number of options, which may or may not be mutually exclusive. Checkboxes are created as follows:

```
Checkbox checkbox1 = new Checkbox("Box 1", null, true);
Checkbox checkbox2 = new Checkbox("Box 2", null, false);
Checkbox checkbox3 = new Checkbox("Box 3", null, false);
Checkbox checkbox4 = new Checkbox("Box 4", null, false);
Checkbox checkbox5 = new Checkbox("Box 5", null, false);
```

In this example, the checkboxes represent choices that are not mutually exclusive, and hence their group parameter is null. The first checkbox's state is set to true, and so it will be checked.

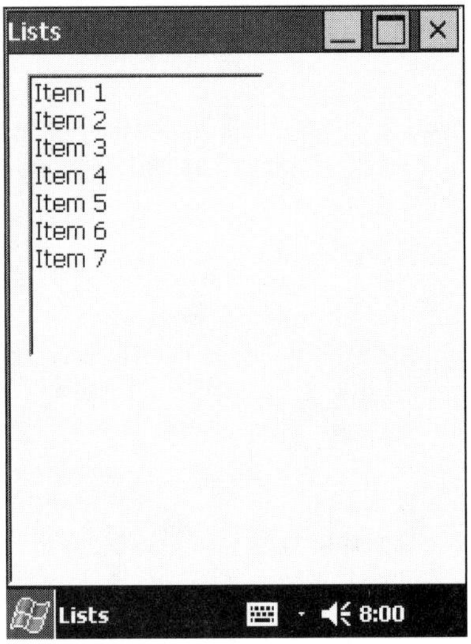

Figure 5.33   Lists

This code can be put into an application as follows:

```
package com.javaonpdas.ui;

import java.awt.*;
import java.awt.event.*;

public class Checkboxes extends Frame {

  public Checkboxes(String title) {
    super(title);
    // handle frame closing events
    addWindowListener(new WindowAdapter() {
      public void windowClosing(WindowEvent e) {
        System.exit(0);
      }
    } );
    // add components
    setLayout(new FlowLayout(FlowLayout.LEFT, 10, 10));
    Checkbox checkbox1 = new Checkbox("Box 1", null, true);
    Checkbox checkbox2 = new Checkbox("Box 2", null, false);
    Checkbox checkbox3 = new Checkbox("Box 3", null, false);
    Checkbox checkbox4 = new Checkbox("Box 4", null, false);
    Checkbox checkbox5 = new Checkbox("Box 5", null, false);
    add(checkbox1);
```

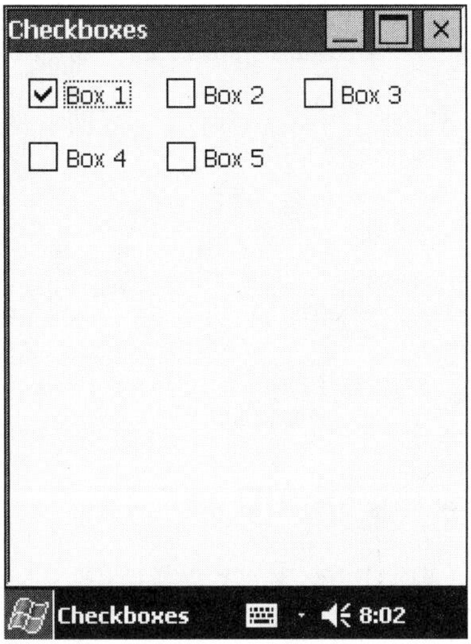

Figure 5.34   Checkboxes

```
    add(checkbox2);
    add(checkbox3);
    add(checkbox4);
    add(checkbox5);
  }

  public static void main(String[] args) {
    Frame f = new Checkboxes("Checkboxes");
    f.setSize(f.getToolkit().getScreenSize());
    f.show();
  }
}
```

Figure 5.34 shows the display on the PocketPC.

FileDialog

The FileDialog uses the standard file choosing dialog for the platform, for the purpose of identifying a file to open or a directory in which to save a file. The dialog object can then be queried to find the file selected and the directory. The FileDialog is modal, so the application's main thread blocks while the dialog is displayed:

```
FileDialog dialog =
  new FileDialog(this, "Open a file", FileDialog.LOAD);
```

```
dialog.show();
textField.setText(dialog.getFile());
```

Putting this code fragment into an application:

```java
package com.javaonpdas.ui;

import java.awt.*;
import java.awt.event.*;

public class FileDialogs extends Frame
  implements ActionListener {

  private TextField textField = null;

  public FileDialogs(String title) {
    super(title);
    // handle frame closing events
    addWindowListener(new WindowAdapter() {
      public void windowClosing(WindowEvent e) {
        System.exit(0);
      }
    } );
    // add components
    setLayout(new FlowLayout(FlowLayout.LEFT, 10, 10));
    Button button = new Button("Open");
    add(button);
    textField = new TextField(20);
    add(textField);
    button.addActionListener(this);
  }

  public void actionPerformed(ActionEvent evt) {
    FileDialog dialog = new FileDialog(this, "Open a file",
      FileDialog.LOAD);
    dialog.show();
    textField.setText(dialog.getFile());
  }

  public static void main(String[] args) {
    Frame f = new FileDialogs("FileDialogs");
    f.setSize(f.getToolkit().getScreenSize());
    f.show();
  }
}
```

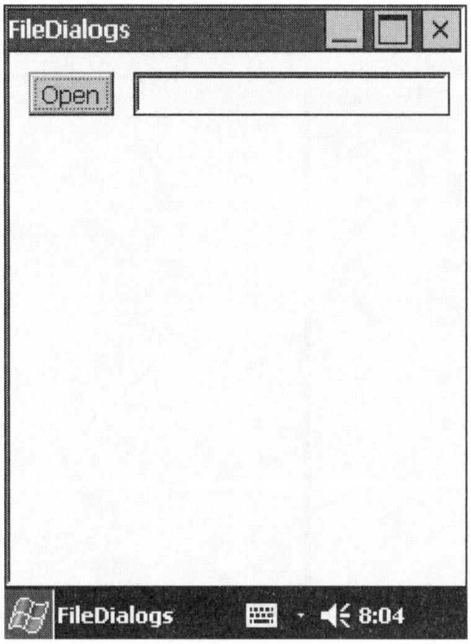

Figure 5.35 FileDialogs

And displaying the application on the PocketPC, we have the application window shown in Figure 5.35.

Pressing the Open button, the FileDialog is displayed as shown in Figure 5.36.

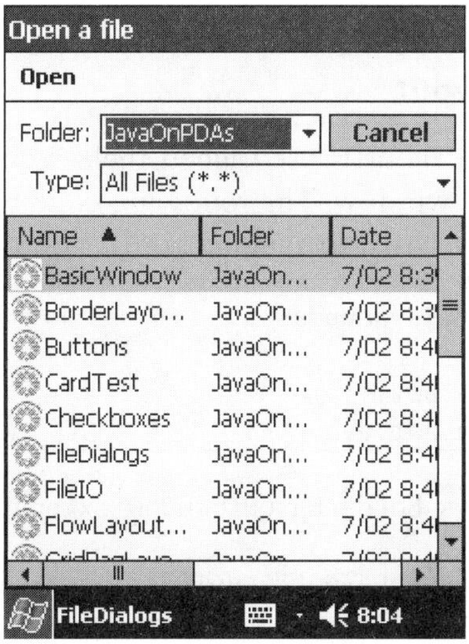

Figure 5.36 Open file dialog

Figure 5.37   The selected file name

On selecting the `Buttons.lnk` file, the `FileDialog` closes and the selected filename is displayed in the text field, as shown in Figure 5.37.

Layouts

PersonalJava supports the full set of AWT layouts.

BorderLayout

The BorderLayout is used when the screen components are arranged along edges of the window. The following code for a simple application shows the BorderLayout used to arrange buttons on the main window (Figure 5.38).

```
package com.javaonpdas.ui;

import java.awt.*;
import java.awt.event.*;

public class BorderLayoutWindow extends Frame {

  public BorderLayoutWindow(String title) {
    super(title);
    // handle frame closing events
    addWindowListener(new WindowAdapter() {
```

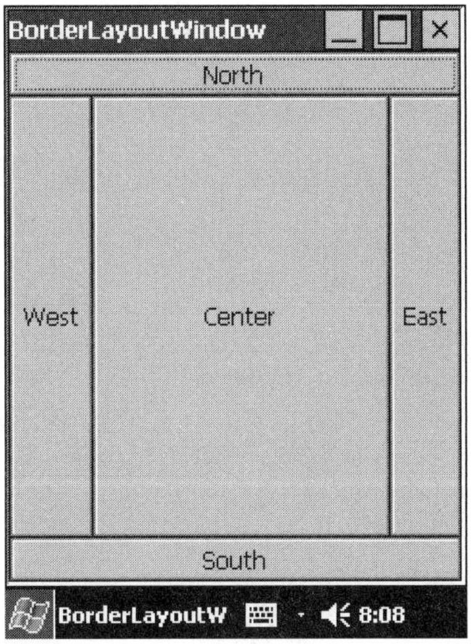

Figure 5.38 BorderLayoutWindow

```
    public void windowClosing(WindowEvent e) {
      System.exit(0);
    }
  } );
  // add components
  setLayout(new BorderLayout());
  add("North",  new Button("North"));
  add("South",  new Button("South"));
  add("East",   new Button("East"));
  add("West",   new Button("West"));
  add("Center", new Button("Center"));
  }

  public static void main(String[] args) {
    Frame f = new BorderLayoutWindow("BorderLayoutWindow");
    f.setSize(f.getToolkit().getScreenSize());
    f.show();
  }
}
```

CardLayout

The CardLayout is used to display a series of screens, one at a time. The result is a component that acts as a stack of cards.

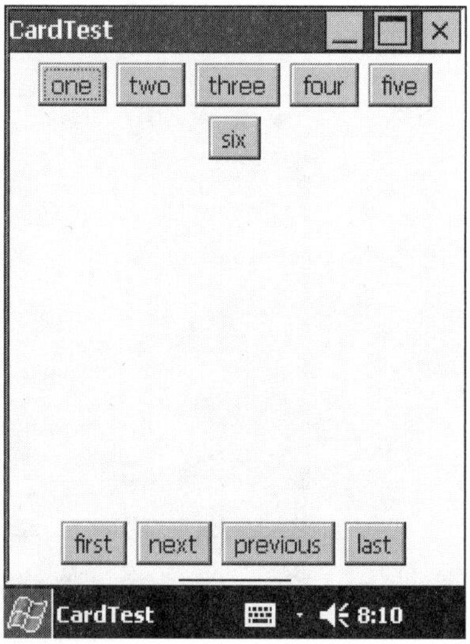

Figure 5.39 CardTest

To demonstrate the CardLayout on the PocketPC, we can use the application CardTest.java, which is included in the JDK 1.1.8 demo directory. The main window is shown in Figure 5.39. Only one modification was necessary to make it work. In the main() method, rather than

```
f.setSize(300, 300);
```

it works better on the PocketPC if we set the frame's size to be the screen size, as follows:

```
f.setSize(f.getToolkit().getScreenSize());
```

FlowLayout

The FlowLayout is used to display screen components on a line in a left-to-right flow, with the components being centered on the line, as shown in Figure 5.40.

```
package com.javaonpdas.ui;

import java.awt.*;
import java.awt.event.*;

public class FlowLayoutWindow extends Frame {
```

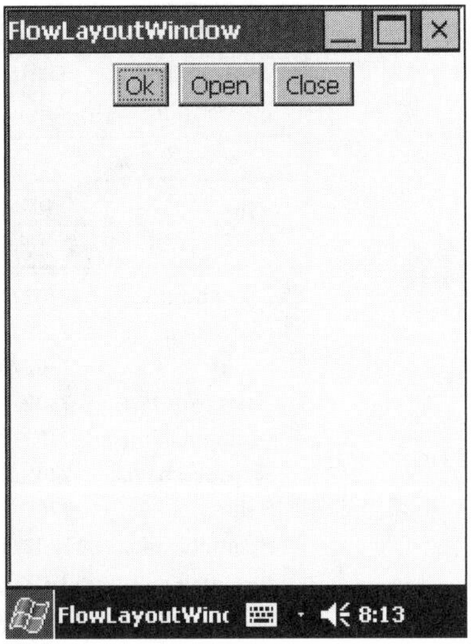

Figure 5.40   FlowLayoutWindow

```java
public FlowLayoutWindow(String title) {
  super(title);
  // handle frame closing events
  addWindowListener(new WindowAdapter() {
    public void windowClosing(WindowEvent e) {
      System.exit(0);
    }
  } );
  // add components
  setLayout(new FlowLayout());
  Button button1 = new Button("Ok");
  Button button2 = new Button("Open");
  Button button3 = new Button("Close");
  add(button1);
  add(button2);
  add(button3);
}

public static void main(String[] args) {
  Frame f = new FlowLayoutWindow("FlowLayoutWindow");
  f.setSize(f.getToolkit().getScreenSize());
  f.show();
}
}
```

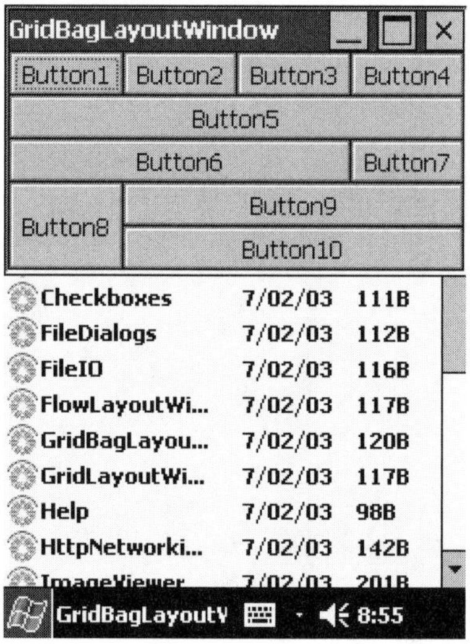

Figure 5.41   GridBagLayoutWindow

GridBagLayout

The GridBagLayout is used to display components in a dynamic grid, where
the components do not need to be of equal size, as shown in Figure 5.41.

```
package com.javaonpdas.ui;

import java.awt.*;
import java.awt.event.*;

public class GridBagLayoutWindow extends Frame {

  protected void makebutton(String name,
                            GridBagLayout gridbag,
                            GridBagConstraints c) {
    Button button = new Button(name);
    gridbag.setConstraints(button, c);
    add(button);
  }

  public GridBagLayoutWindow(String title) {
    super(title);
    // handle frame closing events
    addWindowListener(new WindowAdapter() {
```

```
      public void windowClosing(WindowEvent e) {
        System.exit(0);
      }
    } );
    // add components
    GridBagLayout gridbag = new GridBagLayout();
    GridBagConstraints c = new GridBagConstraints();
    setFont(new Font("Helvetica", Font.PLAIN, 14));
    setLayout(gridbag);
    c.fill = GridBagConstraints.BOTH;
    c.weightx = 1.0;
    makebutton("Button1", gridbag, c);
    makebutton("Button2", gridbag, c);
    makebutton("Button3", gridbag, c);
    c.gridwidth = GridBagConstraints.REMAINDER;
    makebutton("Button4", gridbag, c);
    c.weightx = 0.0;
    makebutton("Button5", gridbag, c);
    c.gridwidth = GridBagConstraints.RELATIVE;
    makebutton("Button6", gridbag, c);
    c.gridwidth = GridBagConstraints.REMAINDER;
    makebutton("Button7", gridbag, c);
    c.gridwidth = 1;
    c.gridheight = 2;
    c.weighty = 1.0;
    makebutton("Button8", gridbag, c);
    c.weighty = 0.0;
    c.gridwidth = GridBagConstraints.REMAINDER;
    c.gridheight = 1;
    makebutton("Button9", gridbag, c);
    makebutton("Button10", gridbag, c);
  }

  public static void main(String[] args) {
    Frame f = new GridBagLayoutWindow("GridBagLayoutWindow");
    f.pack();
    f.setSize(f.getPreferredSize());
    f.show();
  }
}
```

GridLayout

The GridLayout is used to display screen components in a rectangular grid, where each component is of equal size, as shown in Figure 5.42.

Figure 5.42   GridLayoutWindow

```
package com.javaonpdas.ui;

import java.awt.*;
import java.awt.event.*;

public class GridLayoutWindow extends Frame {

  public GridLayoutWindow(String title) {
    super(title);
    // handle frame closing events
    addWindowListener(new WindowAdapter() {
      public void windowClosing(WindowEvent e) {
        System.exit(0);
      }
    } );
    // add components
    setLayout(new GridLayout(3,2));
    add(new Button("1"));
    add(new Button("2"));
    add(new Button("3"));
    add(new Button("4"));
    add(new Button("5"));
    add(new Button("6"));
  }
```

```
public static void main(String[] args) {
  Frame f = new GridLayoutWindow("GridLayoutWindow");
  f.pack();
  f.setSize(f.getToolkit().getScreenSize());
  f.show();
}
}
```

Menus

Menus are a common way of organizing command selections in an application. The MenuWindow application demonstrates how menus appear on the PocketPC. A drop-down menu is shown in Figure 5.43.

```
package com.javaonpdas.ui;

import java.awt.*;
import java.awt.event.*;

public class MenuWindow extends Frame {

  public MenuWindow(String title) {
    super(title);
    // handle frame closing events
```

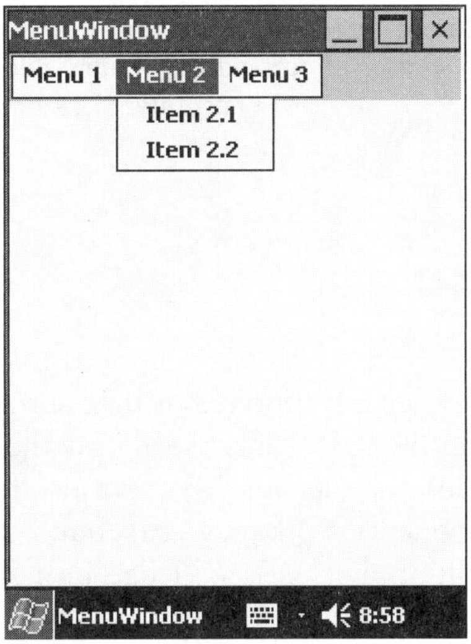

Figure 5.43 MenuWindow

```
      addWindowListener(new WindowAdapter() {
        public void windowClosing(WindowEvent e) {
          System.exit(0);
        }
      } );
      // add components
      MenuBar menuBar = new MenuBar();
      setMenuBar(menuBar);
      Menu menu1 = new Menu("Menu 1");
      Menu menu2 = new Menu("Menu 2");
      Menu menu3 = new Menu("Menu 3");
      menuBar.add(menu1);
      menuBar.add(menu2);
      menuBar.add(menu3);
      MenuItem item11 = new MenuItem("Item 1.1");
      MenuItem item12 = new MenuItem("Item 1.2");
      MenuItem item21 = new MenuItem("Item 2.1");
      MenuItem item22 = new MenuItem("Item 2.2");
      MenuItem item31 = new MenuItem("Item 3.1");
      MenuItem item32 = new MenuItem("Item 3.2");
      menu1.add(item11);
      menu1.add(item12);
      menu2.add(item21);
      menu2.add(item22);
      menu3.add(item31);
      menu3.add(item32);
    }

    public static void main(String[] args) {
      Frame f = new MenuWindow("MenuWindow");
      f.setSize(f.getToolkit().getScreenSize());
      f.show();
    }
  }
```

Summary

In this chapter we have looked at the user interfaces that can be constructed on PDAs with J2ME. We have seen how the implementations render UI components on different devices. We have also become familiar with how to control UI components so that we can build a useful application in Java on a PDA. We will apply this knowledge in a subsequent chapter, but, first, we will explore some other aspects of Java programming on PDAs.

CHAPTER 6

Storing Information

Because a PDA may not always be connected to a server from which to retrieve information, storing information on the local device is important. In this chapter, we will explore the means by which J2ME applications on Palm devices and PocketPCs can store information.

Storing Information Using MIDP

The MIDP provides a set of simple database APIs for storing information on the device. The set of APIs is called the Record Management System (RMS). The APIs include methods to create, update, search, and delete databases.

The underlying implementation of the database is left to the MIDP implementation on the device. On the Palm device, the RMS database is implemented under the covers as a Palm OS database.

In this section, we will have a look at how we use the RMS APIs to store information on the Palm device.

The RMS APIs

The RMS APIs are in the MIDP package javax.microedition.rms. The central class in the package is the RecordStore class, which represents an RMS record store. The `RecordStore` class is used to perform all the operations on the record store. The operations allow the developer to

- Create, open, close, or delete a record store.
- Add a new record, delete a record, and iterate over the records. Filters and comparators can be set up so that the records are sorted and filtered if as desired.
- Obtain information about the record store, such as the number of records, its size, the amount of memory remaining for the record store, its name, the time it was last modified, and the number of times it has been modified (i.e., its version).
- Set up a listener on a record so that a notification is received when the record is modified.

To create and open a new record store, we use the static method `open-RecordStore` on a `RecordStore` object:

```
store = RecordStore.openRecordStore(recordStoreName, true);
```

The second parameter of `openRecordStore` is a Boolean flag to indicate whether we want to be notified if the record store does not already exist. If the flag is true, `openRecordStore` will create a new record store if it cannot find one to open, and open it, returning a reference to the object representing the new store. Note that if the record store is being used by another MIDlet in the same suite, a reference to the open record store will be returned.

If we just wanted to open an existing record store, we could use false for this parameter. In this case, a `RecordStoreNotFoundException` exception would be thrown if the record store did not exist.

To obtain some information about the record store, there are some methods on the `RecordStore` class that can be used:

```
StringBuffer result = new StringBuffer();
result.append("Name: " + store.getName() + "\n");
result.append("Records: " + store.getNumRecords() + '\n');
result.append("Store size: " + store.getSize() + " bytes\n");
result.append("Bytes available: " + store.getSizeAvailable()
                                    + " bytes\n");
result.append("Version: " + store.getVersion() + "\n");
```

To close the record store, we simply call the `closeRecordStore` method on the `RecordStore` object:

```
store.closeRecordStore();
```

Note that every `openRecordStore` method call needs a corresponding `closeRecordStore`. Think of it as a counter that is incremented on an `openRecordStore` and decremented on a `closeRecordStore`. The record store is not actually closed until the counter is zero again.

To remove a record store completely, we use `deleteRecordStore`:

```
RecordStore.deleteRecordStore(recordStoreName);
```

Because a record store can be shared by a number of MIDlets in a suite, it may be possible that another MIDlet is accessing the record store we are trying to delete. In that case, the `deleteRecordStore` method will throw a `RecordStoreException`.

Information is stored in the record store in records, and each record is an array of bytes. The methods to save to and retrieve from a record store all represent the record as an array of bytes. At first glance, having to store information as a byte array may appear to be a cumbersome mechanism. However, with the use of `ByteArrayOutputStream` and `ByteArrayInputStream`, and the corresponding `DataOutputStream` and `DataInputStream`, it is not as onerous as you might think. Say, for example, that you are writing a movie database application for ordering videos or DVDs over the Internet. The basic object you might want to store in a record store could be along the lines of the following:

```
package com.javaonpdas.persistence.rms;

import java.io.*;

public class Movie
  public String title;
  public String actors;
  public long yearReleased;

  public Movie() {
  }

  public Movie(String title, String actors, long yearReleased) {
    this.title = title;
    this.actors = actors;
    this.yearReleased = yearReleased;
  }
```

```
    public String toString() {
        StringBuffer result = new StringBuffer(title);
        result.append(", released ");
        result.append(yearReleased);
        result.append(", starring ");
        result.append(actors);
        return result.toString();
    }
}
```

The MID profile does not define a serialization scheme. As we will see in Chapter 7, "Networking," it is possible to define a simple serialization scheme for sending objects over the network, as well as storing objects in record stores.

In our simple serialization scheme, we define an interface that has two methods:

```
package com.javaonpdas.persistence.rms;

import java.io.*;

public abstract interface Serializable {
  public void writeObject(DataOutputStream dos) throws IOException;
  public void readObject(DataInputStream dis) throws IOException;
}
```

Objects implementing this interface must define an object-specific way to save the state of the object to a `DataOutputStream`, and to retrieve it (and implements serializable to the class definition) from a `DataInputStream`. So, we need to add two methods to our `Movie` class:

```
public void writeObject(DataOutputStream dos) throws IOException {
  dos.writeUTF(title);
  dos.writeUTF(actors);
  dos.writeLong(yearReleased);
}

public void readObject(DataInputStream dis) throws IOException {
  title = dis.readUTF();
  actors = dis.readUTF();
  yearReleased = dis.readLong();
}
```

In this chapter, we will use a `DataOutputStream` with a `ByteArrayOutputStream` underneath to write the object to a record in a record store. In Chapter 7, "Networking," we will use a `DataOutputStream` associated with an `HttpConnection` to send the object over an HTTP connection. The nice feature of our simple serialization scheme is that there is no need to change the definition of the `Movie` class. It is the same, whether it is being used to store movies in a record store or to send movies over an HTTP connection.

Just as we would in J2SE, the way to write objects to a byte stream is to create a `DataOutputStream` with an underlying `ByteArrayOutputStream`:

```
ByteArrayOutputStream bos = new ByteArrayOutputStream();
DataOutputStream dos = new DataOutputStream(bos);
```

Once we have created the `DataOutputStream`, we can pass it to the `Movie` object and tell it to save itself:

```
movie.writeObject(dos);  // write the object to the stream
```

Because the `DataOutputStream` has an underlying `ByteArrayOutputStream`, it is easy to obtain the contents of the stream in the form of an array of bytes:

```
byte[] ba = bos.toByteArray();
```

To add this byte array to the record store, we use the `addRecord` method on the `RecordStore` object:

```
store.addRecord(ba, 0, ba.length);
```

To retrieve an object from the record store, we use a `DataInputStream` with an underlying `ByteArrayInputStream`. Calling the `readObject` method on the `Movie` object reads the byte array from the record and the object is filled with the movie information saved in that record:

```
ByteArrayInputStream bis =
  new ByteArrayInputStream(store.getRecord(recordId));
DataInputStream dis = new DataInputStream(bis);
Movie movie = new Movie();
movie.readObject(dis);
```

To retrieve a collection of records from the record store, RMS provides the `RecordEnumeration` interface. The `RecordEnumeration` provides the ability to search forward and backward over the records in the store. To obtain a RecordEnumeration, call the enumerateRecords method on a RecordStore object:

RecordEnumeration re = store.enumerateRecords(this, this, false);

The first parameter provides the ability to apply a filter on the enumeration. The filter is an object that implements the RecordFilter interface, which means it has a matches method. The matches method returns true if the record is to be included in the enumeration. For example, if we wanted all movies with title beginning with "The," we would write a matches method as follows:

```
public boolean matches(byte[] candidate)
{
  boolean result = true;
  Movie movie = null;
  try {
    ByteArrayInputStream bis = new ByteArrayInputStream(
      candidate);
    DataInputStream dis = new DataInputStream(bis);
    movie = new Movie();
    movie.readObject(dis);
  }
  catch (Exception e) {
    System.out.println(e);
    e.printStackTrace();
  }
  result = movie.title.startsWith("The");
  return result;
}
```

The matches method is called for each record in the record store, providing a byte array to the method to give it the opportunity to test whether it matches the filter criteria. In the example above, we read the movie object from the DataInputStream (with the underlying ByteArrayInputStream) and test whether its title starts with the characters "The". If so, we return true and the record is included in the enumeration.

If no filter object is supplied, then all records in the record store are included in the enumeration.

The second parameter to the enumerateRecords method provides the ability to specify a sort order in the enumeration. If an object that implements the

RecordComparator interface is specified as the second parameter, the interface's compare method will be called for each pair of records in the record store. For example, if we wanted to sort the records by the alphabetic order of the movie titles, we would write a compare method similar to the following:

```
public int compare(byte[] rec1, byte[] rec2)
{
  Movie movie1 = null;
  Movie movie2 = null;
  try {
    ByteArrayInputStream bis1 =
      new ByteArrayInputStream(rec1);
    DataInputStream dis1 = new DataInputStream(bis1);
    movie1 = new Movie();
    movie1.readObject(dis1);
    ByteArrayInputStream bis2 =
      new ByteArrayInputStream(rec2);
    DataInputStream dis2 = new DataInputStream(bis2);
    movie2 = new Movie();
    movie2.readObject(dis2);
  }
  catch (Exception e) {
    System.out.println(e);
    e.printStackTrace();
  }

  // sort by title
  int result = movie1.title.compareTo(movie2.title);
  if (result < 0) {
    return RecordComparator.PRECEDES;
  }
  else if (result > 0) {
    return RecordComparator.FOLLOWS;
  }
  else {
    return RecordComparator.EQUIVALENT;
  }
}
```

For each pair of records in the store (after the filter has been applied), the corresponding pair of byte arrays is passed to the compare method. As before, we can convert the byte arrays to Movie objects. If the title of the first movie object lexicographically precedes the second movie object's title, the compare method returns the predefined constant RecordComparator.PRECEDES. If the title of the first movie follows the second movie's title, the compare method returns the predefined constant RecordComparator.FOLLOWS. If they are the same, the method returns RecordComparator.EQUIVALENT.

If no comparator object is supplied to the enumerateRecords method, the records are sorted in an undefined order.

Code Example

Let's put everything we have covered so far into an example MIDlet and try out a few things. The example below is a simple movie database that uses the serialization technique for saving objects into the record store. It then retrieves them.

```java
package com.javaonpdas.persistence.rms;

import javax.microedition.rms.*;
import javax.microedition.midlet.*;
import javax.microedition.lcdui.*;
import java.io.*;
import javax.microedition.io.*;
import java.util.*;

public class RmsMIDlet extends MIDlet
    implements CommandListener, RecordComparator, RecordFilter {

  private Form mainForm = new Form("RmsMIDlet");
  private StringItem resultItem = new StringItem("", "");
  private Command saveCommand = new Command("Save",
    Command.SCREEN, 1);
  private Command getCommand = new Command("Get",
    Command.SCREEN, 1);
  private Command infoCommand = new Command("Info",
    Command.SCREEN, 1);
  private Command deleteCommand = new Command("Delete",
    Command.SCREEN, 1);
  private Command exitCommand = new Command("Exit",
    Command.EXIT, 10);

  private final Movie[] movies = {
    new Movie("The Patriot",
            "Mel Gibson, Heath Ledger, Joely Richardson",
            2000),
```

```
        new Movie("Gladiator",
                  "Russell Crowe, Joaqin Phoenix, Connie Nielsen",
                  2000),
        new Movie("Swordfish",
                  "John Travolta, Hugh Jackman",
                  2001),
        new Movie("Final Fantasy",
                  "Alec Baldwin, Steve Buscemi",
                  2001),
        new Movie("The Terminator",
                  "Arnold Schwarzenegger, Michael Biehn",
                  1984),
        new Movie("The Matrix",
                  "Keanu Reeves, Laurence Fishburne",
                  1999)};

  public RmsMIDlet() {
    mainForm.append(resultItem);
    mainForm.addCommand(saveCommand);
    mainForm.addCommand(getCommand);
    mainForm.addCommand(infoCommand);
    mainForm.addCommand(deleteCommand);
    mainForm.addCommand(exitCommand);
    mainForm.setCommandListener(this);
  }

  public void startApp() {
    Display.getDisplay (this).setCurrent (mainForm);
  }

  public void pauseApp() {
  }

  public void destroyApp(boolean unconditional) {
  }

  public void commandAction(Command c, Displayable d) {
    RecordStore store = null;
    String recordStoreName = "MyStore";
    try {
      if (c == saveCommand) {
        store = RecordStore.openRecordStore(recordStoreName,
          true);
        for (int i=0; i<movies.length; i++) {
          ByteArrayOutputStream bos =
            new ByteArrayOutputStream();
```

```java
    DataOutputStream dos = new DataOutputStream(bos);
    // write the object to the stream
    movies[i].writeObject(dos);
    byte[] ba = bos.toByteArray();
    store.addRecord(ba, 0, ba.length);
  }
  store.closeRecordStore();
  resultItem.setLabel ("Status:");
  resultItem.setText(movies.length + " records written");
}
else if (c == getCommand) {
  store = RecordStore.openRecordStore(recordStoreName,
    false);
  StringBuffer result = new StringBuffer();
  RecordEnumeration re = store.enumerateRecords(this,
    this, false);
  // RecordEnumeration re = store.enumerateRecords(null,
  //   this, false);
  int i=1;
  while(re.hasNextElement()) {
    ByteArrayInputStream bis = new ByteArrayInputStream(
    re.nextRecord());
    DataInputStream dis = new DataInputStream(bis);
    Movie movie = new Movie();
    movie.readObject(dis);
    result.append(i++ + ": " + movie.title + '\n');
  }
  store.closeRecordStore();
  resultItem.setLabel ("Status:");
  resultItem.setText(result.toString());
}
else if (c == infoCommand) {
  store = RecordStore.openRecordStore(recordStoreName,
    false);
  StringBuffer result = new StringBuffer();
  result.append("Name: " + store.getName() + "\n");
  result.append("Records: " + store.getNumRecords() +
    '\n');
  result.append("Store size: " + store.getSize() +
    " bytes\n");
  result.append("Bytes available: " +
    store.getSizeAvailable() + " bytes\n");
  result.append("Version: " + store.getVersion() + "\n");
  resultItem.setLabel("Info:");
  resultItem.setText(result.toString());
}
```

```
     else if (c == deleteCommand) {
       RecordStore.deleteRecordStore(recordStoreName);
       resultItem.setLabel ("Status:");
       resultItem.setText(recordStoreName + " deleted.");
     }
     else if (c == exitCommand) {
       destroyApp(false);
       notifyDestroyed();
     }
   }
   catch (Exception e) {
     e.printStackTrace ();
     resultItem.setLabel ("Error:");
     resultItem.setText (e.toString ());
   }
}

public int compare(byte[] rec1, byte[] rec2)
{
   Movie movie1 = null;
   Movie movie2 = null;
   try {
     ByteArrayInputStream bis1 =
       new ByteArrayInputStream(rec1);
     DataInputStream dis1 = new DataInputStream(bis1);
     movie1 = new Movie();
     movie1.readObject(dis1);
     ByteArrayInputStream bis2 =
       new ByteArrayInputStream(rec2);
     DataInputStream dis2 = new DataInputStream(bis2);
     movie2 = new Movie();
     movie2.readObject(dis2);
   }
   catch (Exception e) {
     System.out.println(e);
     e.printStackTrace();
   }

   // sort by title
   int result = movie1.title.compareTo(movie2.title);
   if (result < 0) {
     return RecordComparator.PRECEDES;
   }
   else if (result > 0) {
```

```
      return RecordComparator.FOLLOWS;
    }
    else {
      return RecordComparator.EQUIVALENT;
    }
  }
}

public boolean matches(byte[] candidate)
{
  boolean result = true;
  Movie movie = null;
  try {
    ByteArrayInputStream bis = new ByteArrayInputStream(
      candidate);
    DataInputStream dis = new DataInputStream(bis);
    movie = new Movie();
    movie.readObject(dis);
  }
  catch (Exception e) {
    System.out.println(e);
    e.printStackTrace();
  }
  result = movie.title.startsWith("The");
  return result;
  }
}
```

Figure 6.1 shows the result when a new database was retrieved and displayed using the Get button (using a null filter).

If the filter object is supplied to the enumerateRecords method, it filters out all movies with a title that does not begin with "The". Figure 6.2 shows the display in this case.

Figure 6.3 shows the result when the Info button is pressed. Note that the getVersion method returns 25, which is a number that increases for each record that is added, modified, or deleted. It is a useful way to tell whether a record store has changed. Note though that the initial version number is implementation-dependent and is not necessarily zero.

Record Listeners

The RMS API includes the ability to define a record listener object. An object that implements the RecordListener interface can be added as a record listener to a record store, and the interface's notification methods will be called

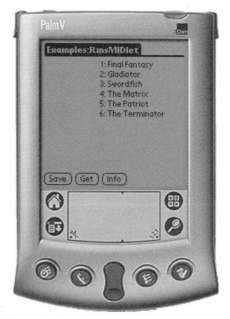

Figure 6.1 RmsMIDlet

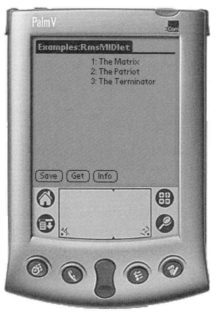

Figure 6.2 Record retrieve with filter applied

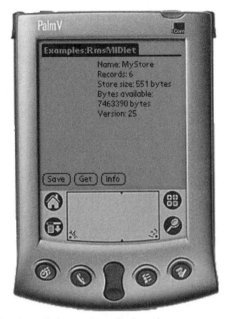

Figure 6.3 RMS database information displayed

when a record in the store is added, updated, or deleted. The listener is registered using the addRecordListener method on the RecordStore object:

```
store.addRecordListener(this);
```

From then until the record store closed, the object referenced by this will be notified when the record store changes. Three separate methods are defined in the RecordListener interface:

```
public void recordAdded(RecordStore store, int recordId);
public void recordChanged(RecordStore store, int recordId);
public void recordDeleted(RecordStore store, int recordId);
```

To demonstrate how this works, we can extend RmsMIDlet to add movie records in a background thread.[1] The MIDlet object is registered as a record listener, which is called each time the background thread adds a new movie record.

---

1. Palm OS does not natively support threads. However, the CLDC mandates support for "green" threads. Green threads are provided by the Java virtual machine, rather than the underlying OS.

First, a new class represents the thread:

```
package com.javaonpdas.persistence.threadedrms;

import java.io.*;
import javax.microedition.rms.*;

public class RmsThread extends Thread {

  int count = 0;
  Movie[] movies = null;
  RecordStore store = null;

  public RmsThread(int count, Movie[] movies,
    RecordStore store) {

    this.count = count;
    this.movies = movies;
    this.store = store;
  }

  public void run() {
    try {
      // add the specified number of movies to the record store,
      // sleeping between adds
      for (int i=0; i<count; i++) {
        ByteArrayOutputStream bos = new ByteArrayOutputStream();
        DataOutputStream dos = new DataOutputStream(bos);
        Movie movie = movies[i % movies.length];
        // write the object to the stream
        movie.writeObject(dos);
        byte[] ba = bos.toByteArray();
        store.addRecord(ba, 0, ba.length);
        // now sleep for a while
        sleep(1000);
      }
      store.closeRecordStore();
    }
    catch (Exception e) {
        e.printStackTrace ();
    }
  }
}
```

This thread class adds a new movie record and sleeps for one second. It repeats this for a specified number of times.

Next, we can define a new `Start` command that starts the thread:

```
Command startCommand = new Command("Start", Command.SCREEN, 1);
...
mainForm.addCommand(startCommand);
...
if (c == startCommand) {
  store = RecordStore.openRecordStore(recordStoreName, true);
  store.addRecordListener(this);
  RmsThread thread = new RmsThread(5, movies, store);
  thread.start();
}
```

Finally, we need to implement the `RecordListener` methods. In this example, we will retrieve the movie record and display the title of records added and updated. Note that trying to retrieve the record specified in the `recordDeleted` method will fail, and an `InvalidRecordIDException` will be thrown:

```
public void recordAdded(RecordStore store, int recordId) {
  resultItem.setLabel ("Status:");
  resultItem.setText("Movie added: " +
    getMovieFromRecord(store, recordId).title);
}

public void recordChanged(RecordStore store, int recordId) {
  resultItem.setLabel ("Status:");
  resultItem.setText("Movie updated: " +
    getMovieFromRecord(store, recordId).title);
}

public void recordDeleted(RecordStore store, int recordId) {
  resultItem.setLabel ("Status:");
  resultItem.setText("Movie deleted: " + recordId);
}
```

And the convenience method `getMovieFromRecord` is defined as follows:

```
Movie getMovieFromRecord(RecordStore store, int recordId) {
  Movie movie = new Movie();
  try {
    ByteArrayInputStream bis =
      new ByteArrayInputStream(store.getRecord(recordId));
    DataInputStream dis = new DataInputStream(bis);
    movie.readObject(dis);
  }
```

```
    catch (Exception e) {
      System.out.println(e);
      e.printStackTrace();
    }
    return movie;
  }
```

Putting it all together, we have the following MIDlet code as follows:

```
package com.javaonpdas.persistence.threadedrms;

import javax.microedition.rms.*;
import javax.microedition.midlet.*;
import javax.microedition.lcdui.*;
import java.io.*;
import java.util.*;

public class ThreadedRmsMIDlet extends MIDlet
  implements CommandListener, RecordComparator, RecordFilter,
  RecordListener {

  private Form mainForm = new Form("ThreadedRmsMIDlet");
  private StringItem resultItem = new StringItem("", "");
  private Command startCommand = new Command("Start",
    Command.SCREEN, 1);
  private Command saveCommand = new Command("Save",
    Command.SCREEN, 1);
  private Command getCommand = new Command("Get",
    Command.SCREEN, 1);
  private Command infoCommand = new Command("Info",
    Command.SCREEN, 1);
  private Command deleteCommand = new Command("Delete",
    Command.SCREEN, 1);
  private Command exitCommand = new Command("Exit",
    Command.EXIT, 10);
  private final String recordStoreName = "MyStore";

  private final Movie[] movies = {
    new Movie("The Patriot",
              "Mel Gibson, Heath Ledger, Joely Richardson",
              2000),
    new Movie("Gladiator",
              "Russell Crowe, Joaqin Phoenix, Connie Nielsen",
              2000),
    new Movie("Swordfish",
              "John Travolta, Hugh Jackman",
              2001),
```

```
        new Movie("Final Fantasy",
                "Alec Baldwin, Steve Buscemi",
                2001),
        new Movie("The Terminator",
                "Arnold Schwarzenegger, Michael Biehn",
                1984),
        new Movie("The Matrix",
                "Keanu Reeves, Laurence Fishburne",
                1999)};

  public ThreadedRmsMIDlet() {
    mainForm.append(resultItem);
    mainForm.addCommand(startCommand);
    mainForm.addCommand(saveCommand);
    mainForm.addCommand(getCommand);
    mainForm.addCommand(infoCommand);
    mainForm.addCommand(deleteCommand);
    mainForm.addCommand(exitCommand);
    mainForm.setCommandListener(this);
  }

  public void startApp() {
    Display.getDisplay (this).setCurrent (mainForm);
  }

  public void pauseApp() {
  }

  public void destroyApp(boolean unconditional) {
  }

  public void commandAction(Command c, Displayable d) {
    RecordStore store = null;
    try {
      if (c == startCommand) {
        store = RecordStore.openRecordStore(recordStoreName,
          true);
        store.addRecordListener(this);
        RmsThread thread = new RmsThread(5, movies, store);
        thread.start();
      }
      if (c == saveCommand) {
        store = RecordStore.openRecordStore(recordStoreName,
          true);
        for (int i=0; i<movies.length; i++) {
          ByteArrayOutputStream bos =
            new ByteArrayOutputStream();
```

```
      DataOutputStream dos = new DataOutputStream(bos);
      // write the object to the stream
      movies[i].writeObject(dos);
      byte[] ba = bos.toByteArray();
      store.addRecord(ba, 0, ba.length);
    }
    store.closeRecordStore();
    resultItem.setLabel ("Status:");
    resultItem.setText(movies.length + " records written");
  }
  else if (c == getCommand) {
    store = RecordStore.openRecordStore(recordStoreName,
      false);
    StringBuffer result = new StringBuffer();
    RecordEnumeration re = store.enumerateRecords(this,
      this, false);
    // RecordEnumeration re = store.enumerateRecords(null,
    //   this, false);
    int i=1;
    while(re.hasNextElement()) {
      ByteArrayInputStream bis = new ByteArrayInputStream(
        re.nextRecord());
      DataInputStream dis = new DataInputStream(bis);
      Movie movie = new Movie();
      movie.readObject(dis);
      result.append(i++ + ": " + movie.title + '\n');
    }
    store.closeRecordStore();
    resultItem.setLabel ("Status:");
    resultItem.setText(result.toString());
  }
  else if (c == infoCommand) {
    store = RecordStore.openRecordStore(recordStoreName,
      false);
    StringBuffer result = new StringBuffer();
    result.append("Name: " + store.getName() + "\n");
    result.append("Records: " + store.getNumRecords() +
      '\n');
    result.append("Store size: " + store.getSize() +
      " bytes\n");
    result.append("Bytes available: " +
      store.getSizeAvailable() + " bytes\n");
    result.append("Version: " + store.getVersion() + "\n");
    resultItem.setLabel("Info:");
    resultItem.setText(result.toString());
  }
```

```
    else if (c == deleteCommand) {
      RecordStore.deleteRecordStore(recordStoreName);
      resultItem.setLabel ("Status:");
      resultItem.setText(recordStoreName + " deleted.");
    }
    else if (c == exitCommand) {
      destroyApp(false);
      notifyDestroyed();
    }
  }
  catch (Exception e) {
    e.printStackTrace ();
    resultItem.setLabel ("Error:");
    resultItem.setText (e.toString ());
  }
}

public int compare(byte[] rec1, byte[] rec2)
{
  Movie movie1 = null;
  Movie movie2 = null;
  try {
    ByteArrayInputStream bis1 =
      new ByteArrayInputStream(rec1);
    DataInputStream dis1 = new DataInputStream(bis1);
    movie1 = new Movie();
    movie1.readObject(dis1);
    ByteArrayInputStream bis2 =
      new ByteArrayInputStream(rec2);
    DataInputStream dis2 = new DataInputStream(bis2);
    movie2 = new Movie();
    movie2.readObject(dis2);
  }
  catch (Exception e) {
    System.out.println(e);
    e.printStackTrace();
  }

  // sort by title
  int result = movie1.title.compareTo(movie2.title);
  if (result < 0) {
    return RecordComparator.PRECEDES;
  }
  else if (result > 0) {
    return RecordComparator.FOLLOWS;
  }
```

```
      else {
        return RecordComparator.EQUIVALENT;
      }
    }

    public boolean matches(byte[] candidate) {
      boolean result = true;
      Movie movie = null;
      try {
        ByteArrayInputStream bis =
          new ByteArrayInputStream(candidate);
        DataInputStream dis = new DataInputStream(bis);
        movie = new Movie();
        movie.readObject(dis);
      }
      catch (Exception e) {
        System.out.println(e);
        e.printStackTrace();
      }
      result = movie.title.startsWith("The");
      return result;
    }

    Movie getMovieFromRecord(RecordStore store, int recordId) {
      Movie movie = new Movie();
      try {
        ByteArrayInputStream bis =
          new ByteArrayInputStream(store.getRecord(recordId));
        DataInputStream dis = new DataInputStream(bis);
        movie.readObject(dis);
      }
      catch (Exception e) {
        System.out.println(e);
        e.printStackTrace();
      }
      return movie;
    }

    public void recordAdded(RecordStore store, int recordId) {
      resultItem.setLabel ("Status:");
      resultItem.setText("Movie added: " +
        getMovieFromRecord(store, recordId).title);
    }

    public void recordChanged(RecordStore store, int recordId) {
      resultItem.setLabel ("Status:");
```

```
        resultItem.setText("Movie updated: " +
          getMovieFromRecord(store, recordId).title);
    }

    public void recordDeleted(RecordStore store, int recordId) {
      resultItem.setLabel ("Status:");
      resultItem.setText("Movie deleted: " + recordId);
    }
}
```

When the MIDlet is executed and the Start button pressed, a movie's title is displayed as it is added to the record store, as shown in Figure 6.4.

Palm OS Implementation of Record Stores

The storage of a record store on the device is implementation-dependent. The implementation of the record store, and even where it is stored, will vary from platform to platform, and is not defined in the MIDP or CLDC specifications. The Palm OS implementation of MIDP uses a Palm OS database to store the record store.

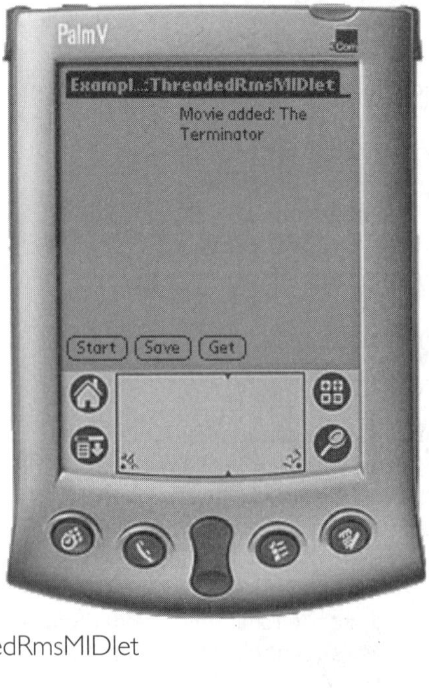

Figure 6.4   ThreadedRmsMIDlet

Although it may be tempting to use this database as you might normally use Palm OS databases, such as to write a conduit that accesses the database and synchronizes the data, there are two important reasons why this is not a good idea:

- The format of the database is not specified or supported, and it may change.
- There are platform-supported ways to transfer information to and from a device. We will look at networking to do this in Chapter 7, "Networking," but basically we will use HTTP to get data to and from the device. Note that this can work whether the Palm device is plugged into the cradle or whether it is connected to a modem over a wireless connection.

This book attempts to support standards where they exist, for the following reasons:

1. Standards make it easier to port an application to other platforms supported by the standard.
2. Standards make it easier for developers to understand what you have written.
3. An application written using a standard makes it more likely to survive future versions of the platform.
4. An application written using a standard makes it easier (and possible) to use new features in future versions of the platform.

For these reasons, accessing the record store database directly is not recommended.[2]

Other Java Databases

If your application requires more than the MIDP RMS provides, you might want to use a third party's database that is compatible with MIDP. Both of the products described in this section provide a MIDP application with JDBC-compatible databases.

---

2. If you are willing to take the risk and write a conduit that reads the record store database anyway, you will find some hints in forum discussions like this one: `http://archives.java.sun.com/cgi-bin/wa?A2=ind0108&L=kvm-interest&D=0&H=0&O=T&T=1&P=49045`.

PointBase

PointBase Micro is an implementation of a subset of the JDBC API found in J2SE, implemented to work in a MIDP environment. The query language is standard SQL. The JAR file is less than 45 KB. The database can be standalone on the device, or synchronized across the network using HTTP to another PointBase product on the server-side called PointBase UniSync.

For more information on PointBase Micro, refer to http://www.pointbase.com/.

ReqwirelessDB

Reqwireless (http://www.reqwireless.com/) is a company that produces several interesting products for J2ME applications. One of those products is ReqwirelessDB. ReqwirelessDB provides access to any JDBC-compliant database from a MIDP application. It does this by providing the JDBC API as a package local to the MIDP application, and a server-side servlet component that performs all the database access.

Storing Information with PersonalJava

Files

Unlike MIDP platforms such as the Palm implementation, PersonalJava platforms such as the PocketPC have a filesystem based on directories and files. With PersonalJava, the developer can therefore make use of the file I/O APIs available in JDK1.1.8.

Reading and Writing a File

Files can be read and written in the same way as in J2SE. For example, a reference to a BufferedReader can be created as follows:

```
file = new File(directory, filename);
in = new BufferedReader(new FileReader(file));
```

As a demonstration of file I/O on the PocketPC, the following simple application displays the FileDialog when the user presses the Open button (Figure 6.5).

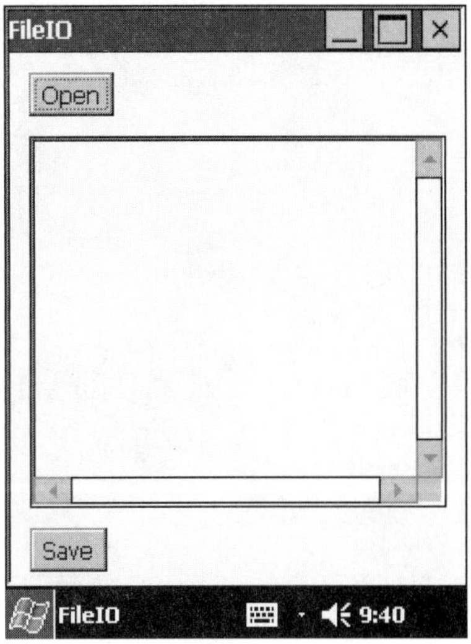

Figure 6.5 FileIO

```java
package com.javaonpdas.persistence;

import java.awt.*;
import java.awt.event.*;
import java.io.*;

public class FileIO extends Frame implements ActionListener {

  TextArea textArea = null;
  Button saveButton = null;
  File file = null;

  public FileIO(String title) {
    super(title);
    // handle frame closing events
    addWindowListener(new WindowAdapter() {
      public void windowClosing(WindowEvent e) {
        System.exit(0);
      }
    } );
    setLayout(new FlowLayout(FlowLayout.LEFT, 10, 10));
    Button button = new Button("Open");
    add(button);
    button.addActionListener(this);
```

```java
      textArea = new TextArea(12,28);
      add(textArea);
      saveButton = new Button("Save");
      add(saveButton);
      saveButton.addActionListener(this);
    }

    public void actionPerformed(ActionEvent evt) {
      String cmd = evt.getActionCommand();
      if (cmd.startsWith("Open")) {
        FileDialog dialog = new FileDialog(this, "Open a file",
          FileDialog.LOAD);
        dialog.show();
        // open and read the file
        String filename = dialog.getFile();
        String directory = dialog.getDirectory();
        BufferedReader in = null;
        try {
          file = new File(directory, filename);
          in = new BufferedReader(new FileReader(file));
          String fileLine = null;
          textArea.setText("");
          for (;;) {
            fileLine = in.readLine();
            if (fileLine == null)
              break;
            else
              textArea.append(fileLine + "\n");
          }
        }
        catch (IOException e) {
          textArea.setText("Error: " + e.getMessage());
        }
        finally {
          try {
            if (in != null) in.close();
          } catch (IOException e) {}
        }
      }
      else {
        // save the text area into the same file
        BufferedWriter out = null;
        try {
          out = new BufferedWriter(new FileWriter(file));
          out.write(textArea.getText());
        }
```

```
      catch (IOException e) {
        textArea.setText("Error: " + e.getMessage());
      }
      finally {
        try {
          if (out != null) out.close();
        } catch (IOException e) {}
      }
    }
  }

  public static void main(String[] args) {
    Frame f = new FileIO("FileIO");
    f.setSize(f.getToolkit().getScreenSize());
    f.show();
  }
}
```

When the user selects a text file, the file is read into the text area on the application's window (Figure 6.6). The user is then able to modify the text in the text area and save the modified text into the same file, by pressing the Save button.

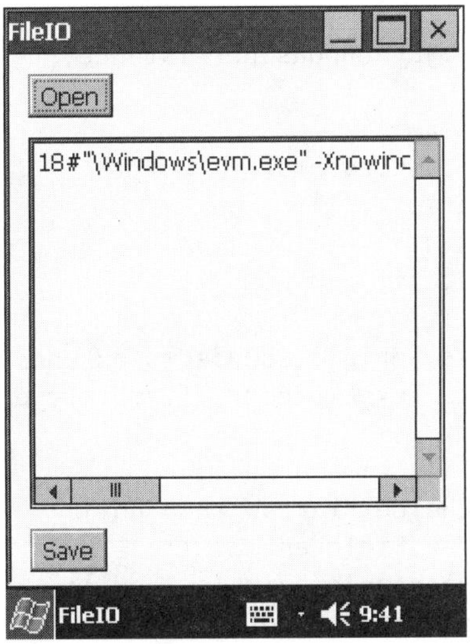

Figure 6.6 The BasicWindow.lnk file

Serializing Objects to a File

PersonalJava supports `ObjectOutputStream` and `ObjectInputStream`, so it is possible to persist objects in the file system.

Suppose we have a `Hashtable` called animals. To write the `Hashtable` to the file system:

```
private static String dataFileName = "animals.dat";
private ObjectOutputStream out = null;
...
out = new ObjectOutputStream(new FileOutputStream(dataFileName));
out.writeObject(animals);
out.flush();
out.close();
```

To read the `Hashtable` from the file system into memory:

```
in = new ObjectInputStream(new FileInputStream(dataFileName));
animals = (Hashtable)in.readObject();
in.close();
```

As an example of this, the following application displays the name of an animal that starts with a selected letter. The animal name can be updated, and it is then saved to a file. If the application is restarted, the previous state of the `Hashtable` is restored from the file.

```
package com.javaonpdas.persistence;

import java.awt.*;
import java.awt.event.*;
import java.io.*;
import java.util.*;
import java.util.zip.*;

public class SerializedObjects extends Frame
  implements TextListener, ItemListener {

  private File file = null;
  private Choice startsWith = null;
  private TextField animalName = null;
  private Hashtable animals = null;
  private static String[] letters = {"a", "b", "c", "d", "e",
                                     "f", "g", "h", "i", "j",
                                     "k", "l", "m", "n", "o",
                                     "p", "q", "r", "s", "t",
                                     "u", "v", "w", "x", "y",
                                     "z"};
```

```
private static String dataFileName =
  "\\My Documents\\JavaOnPDAs\\animals.object";
private ObjectInputStream in = null;
private ObjectOutputStream out = null;

public SerializedObjects(String title) {
  super(title);
  // handle frame closing events
  addWindowListener(new WindowAdapter() {
    public void windowClosing(WindowEvent e) {
      System.exit(0);
    }
  } );
  setLayout(new FlowLayout(FlowLayout.LEFT, 5, 5));
  // add the UI components
  add(new Label("Animal starting with"));
  startsWith = new Choice();
  for (int i=0; i<letters.length; i++) {
    startsWith.add(letters[i]);
  }
  startsWith.addItemListener(this);
  add(startsWith);
  animalName = new TextField(25);
  animalName.addTextListener(this);
  add(animalName);
  // fill the hashtable
  try {
    in = new ObjectInputStream(new GZIPInputStream(
      new FileInputStream(dataFileName)));
    animals = (Hashtable)in.readObject();
    in.close();
  }
  catch (Exception e) {
    animals = new Hashtable();
    animals.put("a", "ape");
    animals.put("b", "bear");
    animals.put("c", "cheetah");
    animals.put("d", "deer");
    animals.put("e", "elephant");
    animals.put("f", "fox");
    animals.put("g", "gorilla");
    animals.put("h", "hippopotamus");
    animals.put("i", "iguana");
    animals.put("j", "jazelle");
    animals.put("k", "koala");
    animals.put("l", "lion");
```

```
      animals.put("m", "monkey");
      animals.put("n", "<<no animal found>>");
      animals.put("o", "<<no animal found>>");
      animals.put("p", "parrot");
      animals.put("q", "<<no animal found>>");
      animals.put("r", "rat");
      animals.put("s", "snake");
      animals.put("t", "tortoise");
      animals.put("u", "<<no animal found>>");
      animals.put("v", "<<no animal found>>");
      animals.put("w", "<<no animal found>>");
      animals.put("x", "<<no animal found>>");
      animals.put("y", "<<no animal found>>");
      animals.put("z", "zebra");
    }
    finally {
      try { if (in != null) in.close(); }
      catch (IOException e) {}
    }
  }

  public void textValueChanged(TextEvent evt) {
    String selectedItem = startsWith.getSelectedItem();
    if (animals.containsKey(selectedItem)) {
      String currentValue = (String)animals.get(selectedItem);
      String newValue = animalName.getText();
      if (!currentValue.equals(newValue)) {
        // update the current key with the selected value
        animals.put(selectedItem, newValue);
        // save the hashtable
        try {
          out = new ObjectOutputStream(new GZIPOutputStream(
            new FileOutputStream(dataFileName)));
          out.writeObject(animals);
          out.flush();
          out.close();
        }
        catch (Exception e) {
        }
        finally {
          try { if (out != null) out.close(); }
          catch (IOException e) {}
        }
      }
    }
  }
}
```

```
public void itemStateChanged(ItemEvent evt) {
  String value = (String)animals.get((String)evt.getItem());
  animalName.setText(value);
}

public static void main(String[] args) {
  Frame f = new SerializedObjects("SerializedObjects");
  f.setSize(f.getToolkit().getScreenSize());
  f.show();
}
}
```

The main window of this application when the letter 'e' is selected is shown in Figure 6.7.

Compressed Files

A useful feature available in J2SE is the ability to wrap the GZIPOutputStream and GZIPInputStream classes around an output and input stream, respectively, in order to automatically compress the data being read and written by the stream. This feature is also available in PersonalJava. GZIPOutputStream is optional in PersonalJava, but the Jeode implementation implements it on the PocketPC.

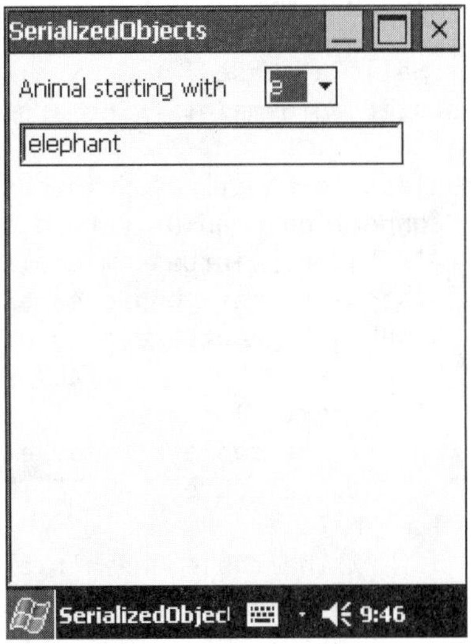

Figure 6.7 SerializedObjects

The following code fragment shows how to compress an object output stream and read from a compressed file as an object input stream.

```
out = new ObjectOutputStream(new GZIPOutputStream
  (new FileOutputStream(dataFileName)));
...
in = new ObjectInputStream(new GZIPInputStream
  (new FileInputStream(dataFileName)));
```

As an example of the effect of compressing an object stream, the animals.object is 395 bytes without compression and 293 bytes with compression.

JDBC Databases

PointBase is a relational database system for small devices running, among others, MIDP on Palm devices and PersonalJava on the PocketPC. It has a footprint of less than 45 KB for MIDP, and less than 90 KB for PersonalJava. It supports username and password security, database encryption, a SQL92 subset including transactions, Unicode, and it uses the underlying persistence of the platform.

The PointBase sample application HelloDatabase connects to a database, tests whether the TEST database exists, either inserts an initial value or updates an incremented value of a counter, and queries the result.

```
import com.pointbase.me.*;

public class HelloDatabase {
    public static void main(String argv[]) {
        try {
            Class.forName("com.pointbase.me.DriverManager");
            Connection conn=DriverManager.getConnection(
                "jdbc:pointbase:micro:test","PBPUBLIC","PBPUBLIC");
            Statement stat=conn.createStatement();
            DatabaseMetaData meta=conn.getMetaData();
            ResultSet rs=meta.getTables(null,null,"TEST",null);
            if(rs.next()) {
                // the table already exists
                stat.execute("UPDATE TEST SET ID=ID+1");
            } else {
                // the table doesn't exist yet
                stat.execute("CREATE TABLE TEST(ID INT)");
                stat.execute("INSERT INTO TEST VALUES(1)");
            }
```

```
                rs=stat.executeQuery("SELECT ID FROM TEST");
                rs.next();
                int count=rs.getInt(1);
                System.out.println("Hello Database!");
                System.out.println("This application was run "+count
                  +" time(s)");
                conn.close();
            } catch(Exception e) {
                e.printStackTrace();
            }
        }
    }
```

To run HelloDatabase, copy pbmicro43.jar from C:\pointbase\lib and HelloDatabase.class from C:\pointbase\samples\micro\HelloWorld\classes to the PocketPC's \My Documents\JavaOnPDAs. Create the HelloDatabase shortcut using the Ant build.xml and copy that to the PocketPC's \My Documents\ JavaOnPDAs as well.

Summary

In this chapter we have examined the record store APIs that the MID profile in J2ME offers for storing information on Palm devices. Although quite simple, the RMS classes provide quite sufficient means to store information between MIDlet invocations, turning the device off and on again, device reboots, etc. The RMS classes are useful for storing information downloaded from an external data source using HTTP, for example. In Chapter 7, "Networking," we will examine the process of transferring data to and from an external data source over HTTP, which complements the discussion here on storing information. Together, the two capabilities of the MIDP can allow the developer to build a versatile data management application.

We have also examined the more powerful persistence mechanisms available to the PersonalJava developer. These include persisting objects to files, and accessing relational databases through JDBC.

CHAPTER 7

Networking

Introduction

The power of the portable information device is that it can roam anywhere, capturing and displaying information along the way. This feature is quite limited, however, if the device has no way of collaborating with other information devices to transfer captured data for analysis, or to retrieve data from a live source for display. By enabling collaboration, networking adds value by an order of magnitude to what the user is trying to achieve. Networking is therefore an extremely important feature of a portable device. Standalone computers were okay in the 1980s, but now we have mobile devices and to get maximum benefit from them they must collaborate with other devices and computers on networks.

In this chapter, we will look at how to perform basic networking on Palm devices using MIDP and on the PocketPC using PersonalJava.

Networking on Palm Devices

The CLDC defines a set of networking APIs called the Generic Connection Framework (GCF). This set of APIs defines the base networking APIs that a CLDC-based profile must support.

While the CLDC specification defines the networking APIs, the profile sitting on top of the CLDC defines the networking protocols available in a particular implementation. The MIDP, for example, uses the CLDC-defined Generic Connection Framework APIs and specifies that any implementation of MIDP must support the http protocol. The MIDP specification states in section 6.1 that "MIDP implementations must support for accessing HTTP 1.1 servers and services."

In this chapter, we will look at how we can connect to an HTTP server, explain how to use the APIs provided in the Generic Connection Framework, and give some working code examples.

The Generic Connection Framework

J2SE has quite a wide and deep set of networking classes. In JDK 1.3, there are 21 classes, six interfaces, and eight exceptions in the networking package java.net. Many of these classes are interrelated and contain much more functionality than a simple portable device requires. This makes it very difficult to create a subset for the memory-constrained devices targeted by CLDC. The designers of the CLDC have generalized the networking features of J2SE, providing a uniform framework for supporting new devices and protocols that devices may require.

For basic networking, J2SE includes the classes such as Socket, HttpURLConnection, DatagramSocket, MulticastSocket, ServerSocket, InetAddress, URL, and URLConnection in the java.net package. Generally, each protocol is handled by a different class. For example, datagrams are implemented using the DatagramSocket class, and HTTP connections are handled by the HttpURLConnection class. However, in J2ME CLDC, the networking classes are quite different. None of the basic networking classes in J2SE exist in J2ME CLDC. Indeed, the java.net package does not exist. The GCF classes are located in a CLDC-specific package, called javax.microedition.io. In the GCF, a single class—the Connector class—handles all the supported networking protocols[1] of the device. The result is that an application's code is essentially the same no matter which protocol is used.

The Connector class has several static methods, which are used to create connections. These methods are summarized in Table 7.1.

The general form of opening a connection is to use a static method on the Connector class, as follows:

```
Connector.open("<protocol>:[<target>][;<parameters>]");
```

---

1. Note that supported protocols are not specified at the configuration level. Specification of the protocols is left to the profiles. This is consistent with the notion that profiles specify features that take advantage of the device's capabilities.

Table 7.1   Methods in the Connector Class

`static Connection open(String name)`	Create and open a connection, using a URL.
`static Connection open(String name, int mode)`	Create and open a connection, using a URL and mode (read, write, or read/write).
`static Connection open(String name, int mode, boolean timeouts)`	Create and open a connection, using a URL, mode, and a flag to raise timeout exceptions.
`static DataInputStream openDataInputStream(String name)`	Create and open a connection data input stream.
`static DataOutputStream openDataOutputStream(String name)`	Create and open a connection data output stream.
`static InputStream openInputStream(String name)`	Create and open a connection input stream.
`static OutputStream openOutputStream(String name)`	Create and open a connection output stream.

The format of the argument to the open method needs to be in accordance with standard URI syntax.[2]

The `<protocol>` part of the parameter string represents the protocol to be used for the connection.

The optional `<target>` part of the parameter is interpreted according to the protocol. For network-oriented connections, `<target>` refers to an address. The address can be a hostname or an IP address. For protocols that are not network-oriented, the `<target>` may be interpreted more loosely. As an example of a protocol that is not network-oriented, in a future profile a supported protocol may be `file:`, and so the `<target>` may refer to the file name.

The optional `<parameters>` part of the string contains a semicolon-separated series of name-value pairs. For example, "`;name1=value1;name2=value2`".

---

2. A URI is a Uniform Resource Indicator. The URI standard is defined in RFC2396, which can be found at `http://www.ietf.org/rfc/rfc2396.txt`. There is also a discussion on URIs in "Java Server & Servlets" by Peter Rossbach and Hendrick Schreiber, Addison-Wesley, 2000.

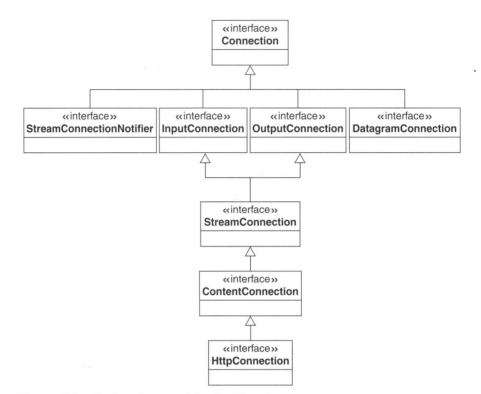

Figure 7.1   Static structure of the GCF interfaces

Even though the MIDP specification mandates http only, http and https are supported in the J2ME Wireless Toolkit 1.0.3 release. The protocols socket, serversocket, comm, and datagram are supplied in experimental form. However, the only protocol provided for the Palm device is the MIDP-mandated http. The positive side of the minimal protocols for the Palm is that the code we write for the Palm will have the best portability across MIDP devices, as http is guaranteed to be available on all MIDP platforms.

Figure 7.1 shows the interfaces specified in the GCF, and how they relate to each other.

Example

To understand the MIDP networking APIs, it's a good idea to look at an example. Let's step through the code from HttpNetworking.java, which is a simple example that downloads a page from a Web server using HTTP.

Example 131

```
private String getPage(String url) throws IOException {
  HttpConnection c = null;
  String result = null;
  try {
    c = (HttpConnection)Connector.open(url);
    DataInputStream dis = c.openDataInputStream();
    byte[] buffer = new byte[(int)c.getLength()];
    dis.readFully(buffer);
    result = new String(buffer);
  }
  catch (Exception e) {
    Alert alert = new Alert("Error");
    alert.setString(e.toString());
    alert.setTimeout(Alert.FOREVER);
    display.setCurrent(alert, mainForm);
    System.out.println(e.getMessage());
  }
  finally {
    if(c != null)
      c.close();
  }
  return result;
}
```

In this simple example, we use a `Connector` to open an `HttpConnection`, which we use to open an input stream. To download the first bytes of the page at the specified URL, we use the `read()` method on the input stream to read the bytes into a byte array. The number of bytes downloaded equals the size of the byte array.

So, what's happening under the covers in this code? First, and perhaps counterintuitively, the HTTP connection is not actually made when the open method is called on the `Connector`. At this point, the `HttpConnection` is considered to be in "Setup" state; the HTTP connection has not yet been made with the server. A connection is made and data is sent and received when one of the following methods is called, causing the `HttpConnection` to transition from the "Setup" state to the "Connected" state:

- `openInputStream`
- `openOutputStream`
- `openDataInputStream`
- `openDataOutputStream`
- `getLength`
- `getType`
- `getEncoding`
- `getHeaderField`

- getResponseCode
- getResponseMessage
- getHeaderFieldInt
- getHeaderFieldDate
- getExpiration
- getDate
- getLastModified
- getHeaderField
- getHeaderFieldKey

To test this example, in the commandAction method of HttpNetworking.java we can use the following code to download the HttpNetworking.html test page, which contains the following:

This is a test page for the HttpNetworking application.

The commandAction method contains:

```
public void commandAction(Command c, Displayable d) {
  try {
    if (c == getCommand) {
      resultItem.setLabel("Requesting page...");
      resultItem.setText("");
      String result = getPage(
        "http://users.bigpond.com/ripple/JavaOnPDAs/↵
HttpNetworking.html");
      // String result = getPage(
      //    "http://192.168.0.3:5555/ripple/JavaOnPDAs/↵
HttpNetworking.html");
      resultItem.setLabel("Received...");
      resultItem.setText(result);
    }
    else if (c == exitCommand) {
      destroyApp(false);
      notifyDestroyed();
    }
  }
  catch (Exception e) {
    e.printStackTrace();
    resultItem.setLabel("Error:");
    resultItem.setText(e.toString());
  }
}
```

When the application is run, we get a screen that resembles that of Figure 7.2.

Example

133

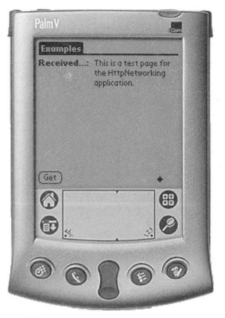

Figure 7.2 HttpNetworking

In our simple example, the connection is made when the openDataInputStream method is called. To look at what's going on under the covers, we can use a tool called tcpmon to look at the exchange between the Palm device and the Web server. The tcpmon tool comes with Axis, a Web services toolkit from Apache that we will be using in a subsequent chapter.[3] We can use tcpmon to set up a TCP/IP tunnel between port 5555 on the hostname localhost and port 80 on the hostname users.bigpond.com where the test page HttpNetworking.html is located. tcpmon will show all the TCP/IP traffic passing through the tunnel.

Note that if you try this on a real Palm device (instead of the Palm Emulator), you will need to use the host PC's IP address in the URL in the source code rather than localhost. The reason is that the Palm interprets localhost as itself, and not the PC. localhost works on the Palm Emulator because all TCP/IP requests are forwarded to the host PC. You can find out the PC's IP address by opening a command line and typing ipconfig. Depending on the PC's configuration, it will display the IP address to the use in the URL. In the following ipconfig response, the IP address to use is 192.168.0.1:

---

3. For some instructions on setting up Axis, refer to "Setting Up Axis and Tomcat" on page 158.

```
C:\>ipconfig

Windows 2000 IP Configuration

Ethernet adapter Local Area Connection:

        Connection-specific DNS Suffix  . :
        IP Address. . . . . . . . . . . : 192.168.0.1
        Subnet Mask . . . . . . . . . . : 255.255.255.0
        Default Gateway . . . . . . . . :

PPP adapter Big Pond:

        Connection-specific DNS Suffix  . :
        IP Address. . . . . . . . . . . : 203.54.22.217
        Subnet Mask . . . . . . . . . . : 255.255.255.255
        Default Gateway . . . . . . . . : 203.54.22.217
```

In this case, you need to change the URL in the `commandAction` method to `http://192.168.0.1:5555/ripple/JavaOnPDAs/HttpNetworking.html`.

On tapping the `Get` button, the `HttpNetworking` application makes the connection and sends the following request:

```
GET /ripple/JavaOnPDAs/HttpNetworking.html HTTP/1.1

Host: users.bigpond.com

Content-Length: 0
```

The Web server replies as follows:

```
HTTP/1.1 200 OK

Server: Microsoft-IIS/5.0

Date: Sun, 08 Dec 2002 05:14:57 GMT

Content-Type: text/html

Accept-Ranges: bytes

Last-Modified: Sun, 08 Sep 2002 07:43:07 GMT
```

Example 135

```
ETag: "82ee595fb57c21:1508"

Content-Length: 55


This is a test page for the HttpNetworking application.
```

How to Recognize Problems

If the Web server is not listening on the port specified in the open method, or if the URL is unreachable, the openInputStream method will throw an IOException.

If the URL is invalid (for example, if we passed "http://illegalurl:5555/index.html" to the open method), the openInputStream method throws a ConnectionNotFoundException.

If the protocol specified is invalid (for example, if we passed "htttp://127.0.0.1:5555/index.html" to the open method), the open method throws a ConnectionNotFoundException, with the message "The requested protocol does not exist htttp://127.0.0.1:5555/index.html."

Finally, if networking is not enabled on the Palm, a helpful message will be displayed when a network connection is attempted, as shown in Figure 7.3.

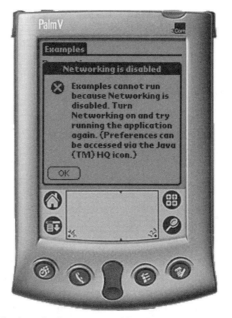

Figure 7.3 Error displayed when networking is not enabled

Internet Access from the Palm Device

Let's have a look at how a J2ME Palm device application can get access to the Internet. The options for connecting a Palm to the Internet are numerous, and vary a little depending on where you live. The following table summarizes the options.

There are three basic options:

1. Connect the Palm to a PC that has Internet access. This can be done by:
   - Direct serial. Connect the Palm in its cradle to a COM port of the PC and use Mochasoft W32 PPP[4] or Windows RAS to connect to the Internet through the PC's modem or network connection.
   - InfraRed. Use a virtual IR COM port such as IrCOMM2k[5] and connect to Mochasoft W32 PPP through the Palm's IR port.
   - Bluetooth. Use the Palm Bluetooth Card to connect to a Bluetooth-enabled PC, such as a Toshiba or Macintosh.
2. Connect the Palm to a mobile phone with an built-in modem to dial an ISP.
3. Connect the Palm to a network that has Internet access. The Palm Bluetooth Card can connect to LAN access points such as Pico, Red-M, and Widcomm.

If you live in the United States, you have all the above options plus one more:

4. Palm.Net. If you have a Palm i705 and live in one of 260 U.S. cities[6] in which Palm.Net has a presence, you can use the i705 to access the Internet.

In this chapter we will look at Options 1 and 2 (direct serial and IR connections, respectively) in step-by-step detail.

Using a Direct Serial PC Connection

To connect the Palm to the Internet using this method, you will need the following:

- Mochasoft's W32 PPP[7]
- Palm cradle connected to the PC's COM port

---

4. Refer to http://www.mochasoft.dk/home.html for more information.

5. Refer to http://www.ircomm2k.de/.

6. Refer to http://www.palm.com/cgi-bin/coveragemap.cgi for a Palm.Net coverage map.

7. W32 PPP does not support connections through a USB cradle or Handspring Visor devices.

Install W32 PPP and set up a new PPP connection over a direct serial connection on the Palm. This is done by selecting System | Preferences, and clicking on the Service | New menu. Name the service "Direct PPP," and select "Direct Serial" as the Connection. There is no need to enter a user name or password. Under Details, select "PPP" as the Connection type, and click OK.

Make sure that the baud rate on the PC is the same as the Connection being used on the Palm. When you start W32 PPP, you should see a window similar to that in Figure 7.4.

To make a connection to W32 PPP from the Palm, go to System | Preferences | Network, select "Direct PPP," and click Connect. Then the Palm is ready to start the networking Java application.

The "Bytes to Palm" and "Bytes from Palm" fields show the number of bytes flowing to and from the Palm, which is a helpful indication that the connection is being made.

Using an IR PC Connection

To use the Infrared connection option, you need the following:

- A Palm with an IR port
- A PC with an IR port

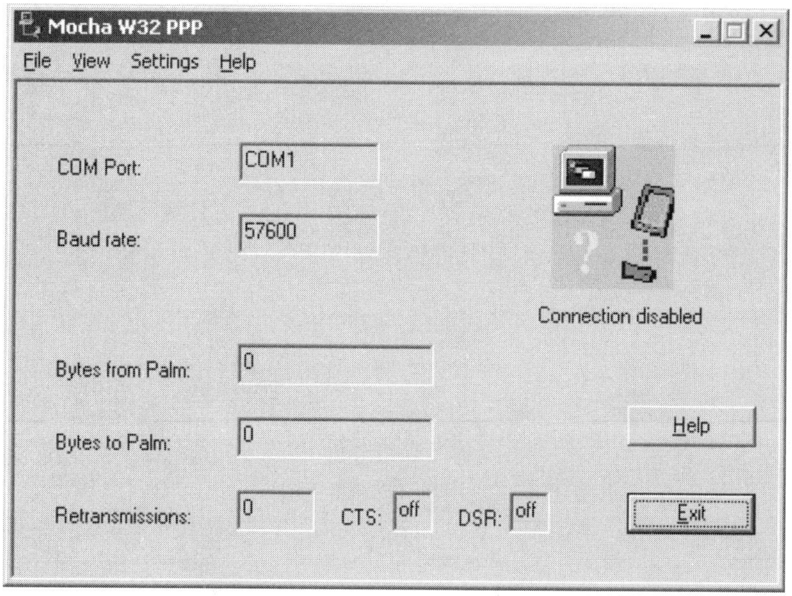

Figure 7.4 Mocha W32 PPP

- IrCOMM2k—Virtual Infrared COM Port for Windows 2000/XP.
- Mochasoft's W32 PPP.

First of all, make sure that the IR port on the PC is enabled. This can be configured into the BIOS settings on the PC. If the IR port is enabled, Windows will display an icon in the Control Panel, as shown in Figure 7.5.

Install IrCOMM2k as described in the instructions. Don't forget to disable the IR port for digital image transfer. IrCOMM2k is installed as a Windows service that emulates a COM port; you will be asked to specify which spare COM port to use. Often, COM4 is a spare port, but this depends on your PC's configuration. Configure W32 PPP to use the COM port being emulated by IrCOMM2k.

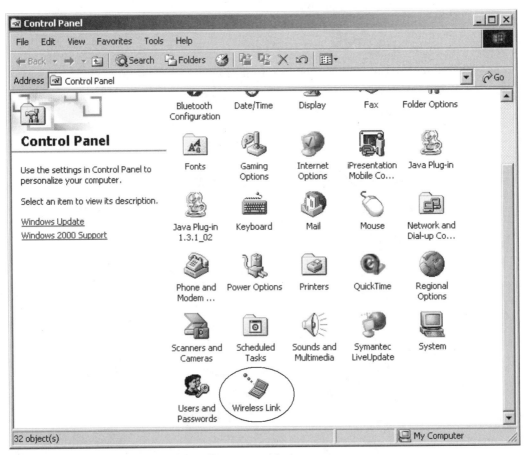

Figure 7.5   Control Panel with the IR port enabled

Using a Mobile Phone Connection

There are two main methods for connecting to the Internet using a mobile phone. The first is by using a data-enabled phone and connecting the Palm OS to the phone using the Infrared port. A data-enabled phone is one that has a built-in modem. For example, Nokia's current list of "data supported" mobile phones is as follows:

- Nokia 8890
- Nokia 8850
- Nokia 8250
- Nokia 8210
- Nokia 8810
- Nokia 7110
- Nokia 6250
- Nokia 6210

Instructions for setting up the Palm OS and the phone for dialing an ISP and making a connection to an ISP are in the user guide for each of the above phones. They can also be found at http://www.nokia.com.

The second method is by using a direct connection cable, such as the GlobalPulse product from TDK. This cable supports a wide variety of phones from Nokia and Ericsson. Refer to http://www.gsm4palm.com for more information.

The following example uses a Palm OS with a Nokia 8210 GSM mobile phone.

First, set up an IR modem connection in the Palm (Figure 7.6). To do this, tap on the Prefs icon and select the Connection menu. Create a new connection and call it IR Modem.

Tap OK. Now go to the Network menu item and set up a service that uses the new IR Modem connection. If you are dialing your ISP, enter the user name, password and ISP phone number into the Network screen (Figure 7.7).

Before a connection can be made, the IR port on the Nokia needs to be enabled. To do this, select Menu | Infrared | Select. The Nokia will display a message saying that Infrared reception is enabled.

To connect, tap on the Palm's Connect button. The Palm will make a connection through the IR port to the Nokia, and the Nokia will dial the ISP and make a PPP connection. Once the connection is made, network applications can access the Internet. To test the connection, start the HttpNetworking application and get the test page. It should work the same way as all the other connection methods.

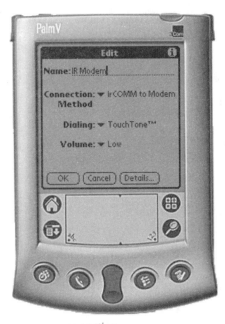

Figure 7.6   Setting up a new connection

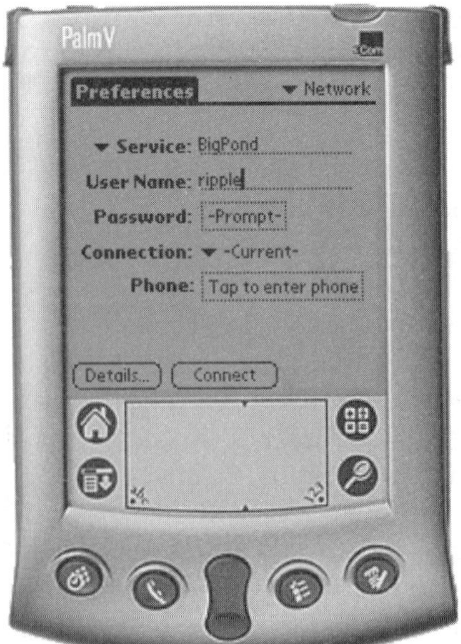

Figure 7.7   Setting up a new network

Networking on the PocketPC

To demonstrate networking on the PocketPC, we will write an application with a very simple user interface. It consists of a button to send the request to retrieve the HTML page, and a text area in which to display the page. The constructor sets it up:

```java
private TextArea textArea = null;
private DataInputStream dis = null;

  public HttpNetworking(String title) {
    super(title);
    // handle frame closing events
    addWindowListener(new WindowAdapter() {
      public void windowClosing(WindowEvent e) {
        System.exit(0);
      }
    } );
    setLayout(new FlowLayout(FlowLayout.LEFT, 10, 10));
    Button button = new Button("Open");
    add(button);
    button.addActionListener(this);
    textArea = new TextArea(12,28);
    add(textArea);
  }
```

Pressing the Open button triggers an `ActionEvent`, sent to the application with an invocation of the `actionPerformed` method.

```java
  public void actionPerformed(ActionEvent evt) {
    String cmd = evt.getActionCommand();
    if (cmd.startsWith("Open")) {
      try {
        URL url = new URL("http://users.bigpond.com/ripple/↵
        JavaOnPDAs/HttpNetworking.html");
        HttpURLConnection c =
          (HttpURLConnection)url.openConnection();
        dis = new DataInputStream(c.getInputStream());
        byte[] buffer = new byte[c.getContentLength()];
        dis.readFully(buffer);
        String result = new String(buffer);
        textArea.setText(result);
      }
      catch (Exception e) {
        textArea.setText(e.getMessage());
      }
```

Figure 7.8   HttpNetworking

```
    finally {
      try {
        if (dis != null) dis.close();
      } catch (IOException e) {}
    }
  }
}
```

Note the use of URL and HttpURLConnection, which are available on Personal Java but are replaced by the GCF in J2ME MIDP on the Palm.

Running the application and pressing the Open button shows a screen like the one in Figure 7.8.

Using a Mobile Phone Infrared Connection on the PocketPC

To use an infrared connection between the PocketPC and a mobile phone, we first need to set up the Generic IrDA modem on the PocketPC. In Settings | Connections, set up a new connection and call it "Mobile Phone" (Figure 7.9).

Select the Generic IrDA modem and the baud rate. Click on Advanced and make sure that Software flow control is selected (Figure 7.10).

Click OK.

Figure 7.9   Setting up the IrDA connection

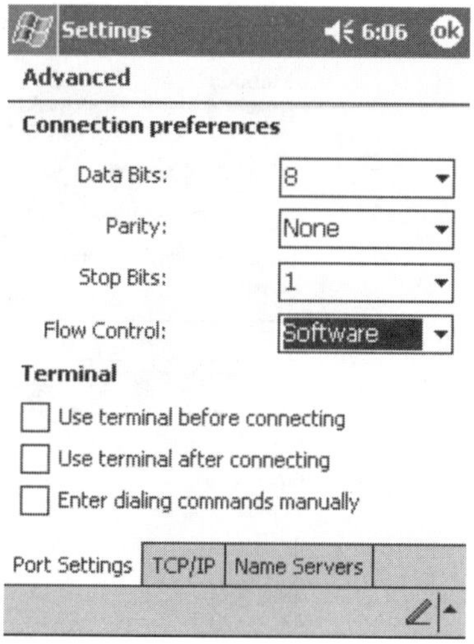

Figure 7.10   Setting software flow control

Now enter the phone number of your ISP (Figure 7.11).

Deselect "Wait for dial tone" (Figure 7.12).

Enable the IrDA connection on the mobile phone. On the Nokia 8210, this is done by selecting Menu I Infrared.

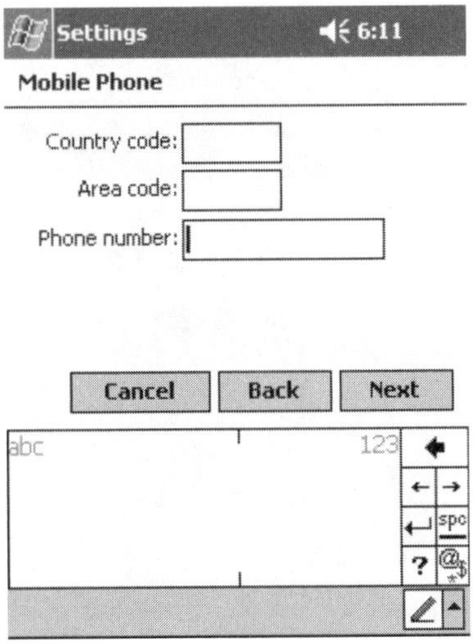

Figure 7.11   Entering the ISP phone number

Figure 7.12   Disabling wait for dial tone

On the PocketPC, make the connection, making sure that the IrDA ports on the two devices are reasonably aligned. The PocketPC should dial the ISP on the mobile phone (Figure 7.13).

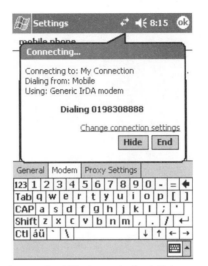

Figure 7.13   Connecting to the ISP through the IrDA port

When the PocketPC is connected to the ISP, it will display the screen as shown in Figure 7.14.

Once a connection to the Internet is made, we can start the HttpNetworking application as before, and press the Open button to retrieve the test HTML page (Figure 7.15).

Figure 7.14   A successful connection to the ISP

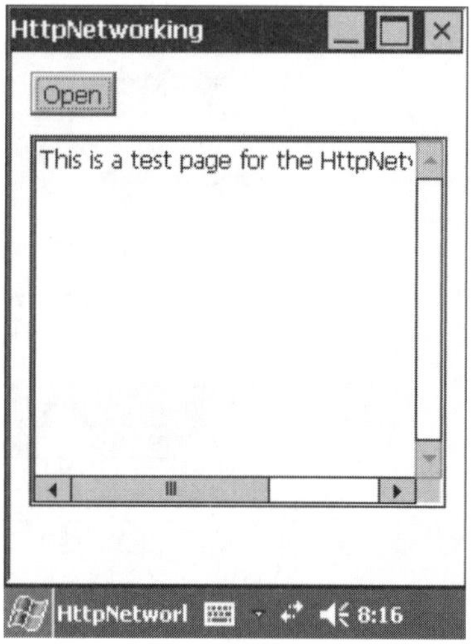

Figure 7.15   Running HttpNetworking with a network connection via the IrDA
port and a mobile phone

Using a Bluetooth Connection on the PocketPC

In a Bluetooth-enabled PocketPC such as the iPaq 3870, it is possible to connect to the Internet through a Bluetooth-enabled PC or network access point.
Note that for many Bluetooth adaptors for PCs running Windows, Internet
Connection Sharing (ICS) must be enabled for the Bluetooth network to
access work.

To connect to the network, turn on the Bluetooth radio and start Bluetooth Manager (Figure 7.16).

Click on the remote Bluetooth device to show its device information
(Figure 7.17).

Click on Actions, and the menu as shown in Figure 7.18 will be displayed.

Selecting Connect to Network Access will connect to the remote device,
with progress shown in the Figure 7.19 popup window.

Once connected, we can start the HttpNetworking application again and
this time retrieve the test HTML page via a wireless Bluetooth connection
(Figure 7.20).

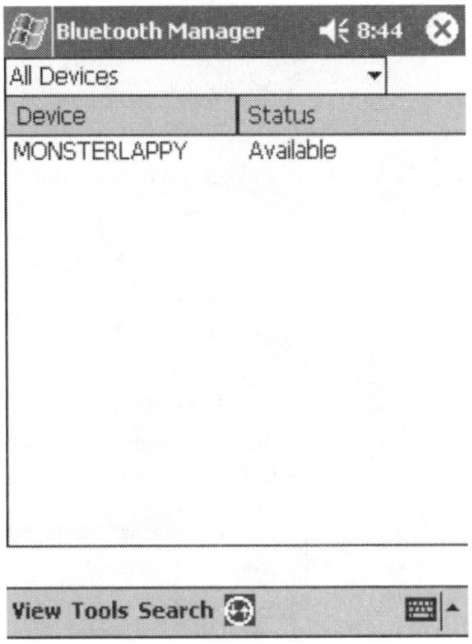

Figure 7.16 The Bluetooth Manager screen

Figure 7.17 Device information for a remote device

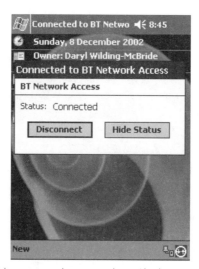

Figure 7.18   The selection of actions available for the remote device

Figure 7.19   Establishing network access through the remote device

Figure 7.20 Running HttpNetworking with a network connection via Bluetooth

Summary

In this chapter we have used basic examples to illustrate the code required to do networking using the CLDC's Generic Connection Framework on the Palm, and PersonalJava networking APIs on the PocketPC. We have made network connections through a direct connection, Infrared, and Bluetooth.

The techniques used in this chapter will be applied and become more interesting in Chapter 8, "Integrating with the Enterprise Using Web Services," where we will see how a PDA using networking functions can collaborate with larger systems to form an enterprise solution.

CHAPTER 8

Integrating with the Enterprise Using Web Services

What Is a Web Service?

A Web service is a self-contained module of application logic that can be exposed to other applications over a network, usually the Internet. A Web service interface hides the technology used to implement the application logic, so that an application implemented in one particular technology can be accessed by using a Web service by another application implemented in a different technology, provided both adhere to the specification of the Web service interface.

There are several competing standards for describing Web services, but the best known is the Web Services Description Language (WSDL),[1] an XML format that describes XML-based services as an abstract set of methods, a binding of these abstract methods to a particular protocol (transport and data format used to invoke them), and the endpoint of the service. A commonly used binding extension to WSDL is SOAP, an XML protocol for invoking a service, usually (but not limited to) using HTTP.

---

1. For an introductory article on WSDL, refer to http://www.ibm.com/developerworks/webservices/library/ws-soap/index.html?dwzone=ws. The WSDL specification can be found at http://www.w3.org/TR/wsdl.

SOAP[2] supports two interaction styles: remote procedure call (RPC) and document literal. RPC style is similar to invoking an object's method to perform some procedural functionality. RPC style is suited to synchronous interactions with a published API. In document style, any XML document can be exchanged. The document need not be limited to the SOAP body specification, and need not be predefined. Document style is suited to asynchronous interactions, where a contract is not necessarily published beforehand.

In this chapter, we will use Web services that are modules of application logic invoked over the network, using SOAP in RPC style over HTTP and described with WSDL.

The benefits of Web services include:

- Messages to and from a Web service are easy to read.
- HTTP is almost always allowed through corporate firewalls.
- Web services promise to be ubiquitous. They are based on XML and HTTP, which are widely supported by a broad range of devices with varying capabilities.
- Just about every vendor supports Web services. Web services are becoming a common mechanism for integrating applications and systems, and tool support for creating them are now in their second generation of maturity.
- They are implementation-neutral. Web services can be implemented in any language on any platform. The server and the client are happily ignorant of the technology or operating system used at the other end of the interaction.

However, there are some limitations (although these will diminish over time):

- In practice, it is not yet straightforward to find a Web service and use it without knowing more about it than what is given in the WSDL file. Implementations vary between servers and clients. Writing a client for a particular Web service is still a matter of trial and error.
- Because they are based on XML, which is rather verbose and takes time and resources to process, Web services are not well suited to extremely constrained devices with limited processing and memory capabilities.

Web services is a vast field, and rapidly expanding. If you want to find out more, a good starting point is IBM's developerWorks (http://www-106.ibm.com/developerworks/webservices/).

---

2. To read the SOAP specification, refer to http://www.w3.org/TR/SOAP/.

In this chapter, we will look at how to access functionality provided by a Web service, both from Palm and PocketPC clients. To get an end-to-end understanding, we will go through the process of developing the Web service, deploying it on the server, and demonstrating several ways of accessing it from a PDA.

The ImageService Web Service

The ImageService Web service is a simple service designed to allow clients to retrieve binary images from the server. There are two methods a client can invoke:

- Get the names of available images. This method returns the names of images available on the server for retrieval.
- Get an image with a specified name. This method returns an object representing the image specified by the client by name.

Since SOAP is based on XML, a textual format, a means by which binary information such as an image can be sent using SOAP must be used. A common mechanism is to encode the image using Base64. Base64 is a standard originally developed for sending binary objects in emails and specified in the Multipurpose Internet Mail Extensions (MIME) standard.[3] Base64 provides a means to encode a binary object into a string, and also to decode the string back into a binary object. This is done by treating each set of three 8-bit bytes of binary data as a set of four 6-bit groups, and mapping each group of six bits to a printable subset of the ASCII character set. Each 6-bit number is used to look up the corresponding character in the Base64 alphabet. Table 8.1 shows the Base64 alphabet.

The characters thus obtained are concatenated to form the encoded string.[4] The string is decoded back into the binary object by the reverse process. If the decoder comes across a character in the string that is not in the Base64 alphabet, the decoder must ignore the character and continue with the next character.

The ImageService interface has two methods:

```
public String[] getNames(String extension);
public ImageValue getImage(String name);
```

---

3. For more information on Base64, refer to the MIME specification http:// www.faqs.org/rfcs/rfc2045.html, section 6.8.

4. In MIME, the encoded string is broken into lines of no more than 76 characters each. In SOAP, this is not required and the encoded string can be continuous.

Table 8.1   The Base64 Alphabet[a]

Value	Encoding	Value	Encoding	Value	Encoding	Value	Encoding
0	A	17	R	34	i	51	z
1	B	18	S	35	j	52	0
2	C	19	T	36	k	53	1
3	D	20	U	37	l	54	2
4	E	21	V	38	m	55	3
5	F	22	W	39	n	56	4
6	G	23	X	40	o	57	5
7	H	24	Y	41	p	58	6
8	I	25	Z	42	q	59	7
9	J	26	a	43	r	60	8
10	K	27	b	44	s	61	9
11	L	28	c	45	t	62	+
12	M	29	d	46	u	63	/
13	N	30	e	47	v		
14	O	31	f	48	w	(pad)	=
15	P	32	g	49	x		
16	Q	33	h	50	y		

a. This is Table 1 from RFC2045 at http://www.faqs.org/rfcs/rfc2045.html.

The getImage method returns an ImageValue object. This is partly to demonstrate how complex objects (versus primitive types) are sent across SOAP. The object has two attributes for the sake of demonstration: a long, representing the date the image was last modified, and a String, representing the Base64 encoded image.

For the purposes of SOAP serialization, the ImageValue supports a Java bean interface style. That is, it has a constructor with no arguments, and setters and getters for its attributes.

The `ImageValue` class is defined thus:

```
package com.javaonpdas.webservices;

public class ImageValue {
  public long dateAsLong;
  public String encodedImage;

  public ImageValue() {
  }

  public ImageValue(long dateAsLong, String encodedImage) {
    this.dateAsLong = dateAsLong;
    this.encodedImage = encodedImage;
  }

  public long getDate() {
    return this.dateAsLong;
  }

  public void setDate(long dateAsLong) {
    this.dateAsLong = dateAsLong;
  }

  public String getEncodedImage() {
    return this.encodedImage;
  }

  public void setEncodedImage(String encodedImage) {
    this.encodedImage = encodedImage;
  }
}
```

The `getNames` method returns a `String` array with the file names of image files with the specified extension in a particular directory. The directory name is hard-coded for the purposes of this example.

The `ImageService` class is listed in the following.

```
package com.javaonpdas.webservices;

import java.util.Date;
import java.io.File;
import java.io.FileInputStream;
import java.io.FilenameFilter;
```

```java
public class ImageService {
  private String directory =
    "C:\\JavaOnPDAs\\Desktop\\resources";
  public ImageValue getImage(String name) {
    String encodedImage = null;
    long timeStamp = 0;
    FileInputStream fis = null;
    try {
      // read the file into a byte array
      File imageFile = new File(directory + "\\" + name);
      if (imageFile.exists()) {
        timeStamp = imageFile.lastModified();
        fis = new FileInputStream(imageFile);
        int length = fis.available();
        byte[] rawImage = new byte[length];
        fis.read(rawImage);
        // encode the byte array into a Base64 string
        encodedImage = org.apache.axis.encoding.Base64.encode(
          rawImage);
      }
    }
    catch (Exception e) {
      System.out.println("Error:" + e);
    }
    finally {
      try { if (fis != null) fis.close(); }
      catch (Exception e) {}
    }
    ImageValue image = new ImageValue(timeStamp, encodedImage);
    return image;
  }

  public String[] getNames(String extension) {
    final String ext = extension;
    FilenameFilter filter = new FilenameFilter() {
      public boolean accept(File dir, String name) {
        return name.endsWith(ext);
      }
    };
    File dir = new File(directory);
    String[] files = dir.list(filter);
    return files;
  }
}
```

Some important points about this code:

- Since the Web service will be deployed on Axis, we will make use of the built-in Base64 class with a static encode method, `org.apache.axis.encoding.Base64`.
- This is a "normal" Java class definition. Apart from making use of the Axis `Base64` class (which could be replaced by any Base64 encoder), there is nothing here to suggest that this class will be deployed as a Web service. The publication of this class's methods as a Web service interface is completely separate to the class definition.

Now that we have a class that will serve as our Web service, the next step is to write a Web service deployment descriptor (WSDD). Web service deployment descriptors conform to a standard XSD.

For our `ImageService` class, the WSDD is quite simple. The WSDD describes:

- The name of the Web service.
- The class of the Web service.
- The methods of the class that are allowed to be accessed.
- That the service uses the built-in bean serializer for converting an object to a SOAP representation, by accessing its attributes and converting those base types to SOAP format.
- The name of the class to serialize, using the bean serializer.

The WSDD for the `ImageService` Web service is `deploy-ImageService-AXIS.wsdd`, and looks like this:

```
<deployment xmlns="http://xml.apache.org/axis/wsdd/"
       xmlns:java="http://xml.apache.org/axis/wsdd/providers/java">

   service name="ImageService" provider="java:RPC">
      parameter name="className"
         value="com.javaonpdas.webservices.ImageService"/>
      <parameter name="allowedMethods" value="*"/>
      <beanMapping qname="ns:ImageValue"
         xmlns:ns="urn:BeanService"
         languageSpecificType=
            "java:com.javaonpdas.webservices.ImageValue"/>
   </service>

</deployment>
```

Now we're ready to set up Axis and Tomcat, which we will use to deploy and test the `ImageService` Web service.

Setting Up Axis and Tomcat

Axis (http://xml.apache.org/axis/index.html) is an Apache XML open source project, and is the successor to Apache SOAP, one of the earliest SOAP implementations. Axis is a Java implementation of a SOAP server and client. Axis operates within an application server or servlet engine, and one of the most popular servlet engines is another Apache open source project, Tomcat (http://jakarta.apache.org/tomcat/index.html). Tomcat is the reference implementation of the Java Server Pages (JSP) 1.2 and Servlet 2.3 specifications. Axis can use just about any servlet engine, provided it supports version 2.2 (or greater) of the servlet specification.

Download Axis from http://xml.apache.org/axis/releases.html. The examples in this book use Axis 1.0.

Download Tomcat from http://jakarta.apache.org/builds/jakarta-tomcat-4.0/release/v4.1.12/. The examples in this book use Tomcat 4.1.

Tomcat Installation[5]

Unzip the Tomcat binary package into a convenient location. We will refer to this location as ${tomcat-base}. Change to the directory ${tomcat-base}\bin, and run the batch file startup.cmd to start Tomcat.

By default, Tomcat runs on port 8080. As Tomcat is starting, you should see information similar to the following:

```
16/11/2002 13:36:29 org.apache.commons.modeler.Registry loadRegistry
INFO: Loading registry information
16/11/2002 13:36:30 org.apache.commons.modeler.Registry getRegistry
INFO: Creating new Registry instance
16/11/2002 13:36:31 org.apache.commons.modeler.Registry getServer
INFO: Creating MBeanServer
16/11/2002 13:36:32 org.apache.coyote.http11.Http11Protocol init
INFO: Initializing Coyote HTTP/1.1 on port 8080
Starting service Tomcat-Standalone
Apache Tomcat/4.1.10
16/11/2002 13:36:43 org.apache.coyote.http11.Http11Protocol start
INFO: Starting Coyote HTTP/1.1 on port 8080
16/11/2002 13:36:43 org.apache.jk.common.ChannelSocket init
INFO: JK2: ajp13 listening on tcp port 8009
16/11/2002 13:36:43 org.apache.jk.server.JkMain start
```

---

5. This section assumes that you have already installed JDK 1.4, and that JAVA_HOME is pointing to it.

```
INFO: Jk running ID=0 time=10/90  config=C:\jakarta-tomcat-
4.1.10\bin\..\conf\jk2.properties
```
Once Tomcat has started, test that it is working by pointing your browser to `http://localhost:8080/`. You should see something similar to Figure 8.1. To shut down Tomcat, run the `shutdown.cmd` batch file.

Axis Installation

Unzip the Axis ZIP file into a convenient location. We will refer to this location as `${axis-base}`. In the directory `${axis-base}\webapps`, there is a directory called axis. This directory contains the Axis Web application, which can be copied over to the webapps directory of the servlet engine (Tomcat, in this case). So, copy `${axis-base}\webapps\axis` to `${tomcat-base}\webapps`.

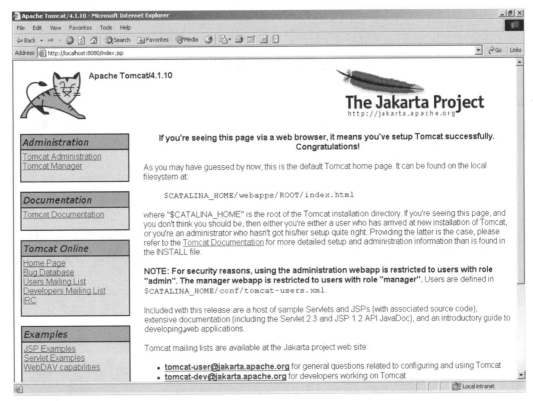

Figure 8.1 The Tomcat test page

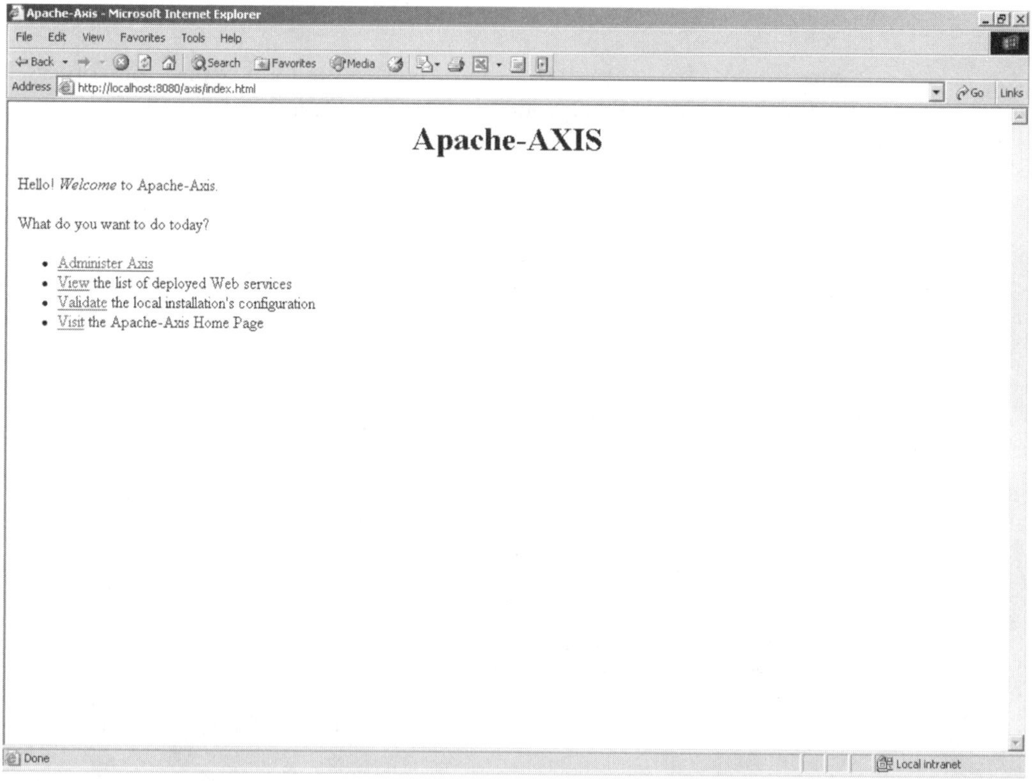

Figure 8.2   The Axis test page

To test the installation, point your browser to http://127.0.0.1:8080/
axis/. You should see a page similar to Figure 8.2.

Check whether AXIS is properly configured and that it can find all the
components it requires by clicking on the Validate link. You should see a
page like that shown in Figure 8.3.

Note that the page should say that all the needed components can be
found.

Now we are ready to deploy the Web service.

Deploying the ImageService Web Service

In Tomcat, each Web application has a WEB-INF subdirectory, in which class
files or JAR files specific to the application are located. This is done so that each
Web application can have a set of components (classes or JAR files) independent of other Web applications on the same instance of Tomcat. Axis will

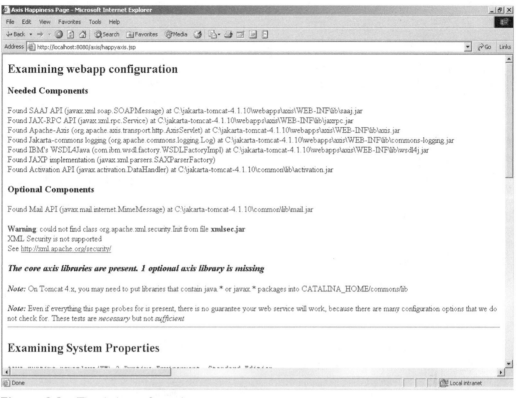

Figure 8.3 The Axis configuration page

need to find our Web service class, so we need to bundle a JAR file and put it in our Web application's lib directory. This is done with the CompileDesktop target in the Ant build file:

```
<target name="CompileDesktop" depends="Init">
  <!-- Compile the Desktop source code -->
  <javac
    srcdir="${desktopsrc}"
    destdir="${desktopdest}"
    debug="off">
    <classpath>
      <pathelement path="${desktopdest}"/>
      <path refid="axis.path"/>
    </classpath>
  </javac>
  <jar jarfile="${desktoplib}\javaonpdas-desktop.jar"
```

```
                basedir="${desktopdest}"
                includes="**\*.class"
        />
        <copy file="${desktoplib}\javaonpdas-desktop.jar"
                todir="${axis-webapp}" />
        <copy file="${desktoplib}\javaonpdas-desktop.jar"
                todir="${proxy-webapp}" />
    </target>
```

This target compiles all the source files under the desktop directory, creates the JAR javaonpdas-desktop.jar, and copies it to the Axis webapp directory. Stop Axis and start it again to make sure it has seen the new JAR file.

Now that Axis can see the classes that implement the Web service, we can deploy it.

Deploying the Web Service

In this step we make use of the deployment descriptor we prepared previously. Axis has a deployment client that we will use, which is org.apache.axis. client.AdminClient. The Ant build target DeployImageService performs this task:

```
    <target name="DeployImageService" depends="CompileDesktop">
      <!-- Run the ImageService web service -->
      <java
        classname="org.apache.axis.client.AdminClient"
        dir="."
        fork="true"
        failonerror="true">
        <classpath>
          <pathelement path="${desktopdest}"/>
          <path refid="axis.path"/>
        </classpath>
        <arg line="-l${webserviceadmin} ${desktopsrc}\com\javaonpdas\↵
        webservices\deploy-ImageService-AXIS.wsdd"/>
      </java>
    </target>
```

Running this task will tell Axis about the new Web service:

```
C:\JavaOnPDAs>ant DeployImageService
Buildfile: build.xml

Init:

CompileDesktop:
```

```
DeployImageService:
    [java] - Processing file .\Desktop\src\com\javaonpdas\
webservices\deploy-ImageService-AXIS.wsdd
    [java] - <Admin>Done processing</Admin>

BUILD SUCCESSFUL
Total time: 8 seconds
```

If you see any exceptions thrown during this step, it is likely that Axis cannot find a class referenced in the deployment descriptor. If you do see such an exception, check that the JAR file is in the Axis webapp `lib` directory, and try restarting Axis and redeploying the Web service.

Testing

The first step is to check whether Axis thinks that the Web service has been properly deployed. Point your browser at the main Axis page (http:// 127.0.0.1:8080/axis/index.html), and click the View link. This will display all the Web services deployed on this server, as shown in Figure 8.4.

Click on the WSDL link to display a description of the service and how to invoke it. While the WSDL may seem a bit daunting, it describes the operations (i.e., methods) of the Web service that can be invoked (getNames and getImage), the transport to use to invoke them (HTTP), and the location of the service (http://127.0.0.1:8080/axis/services/ImageService).

The next step is to test the Web service from a client. To do so from the desktop, the command line application com.javaonpdas.client.ImageServiceClient calls the Web service and calls both methods, displaying information about what is returned.

Using the Axis client (as we will see later, other SOAP clients have slight variations), the steps to calling a Web service are:

1. Set up the Call object. This involves telling the Call object the end point URL, the name of the service, and the method to call.

```
Service service = new Service();
Call getNamesCall = (Call)service.createCall();
getNamesCall.setTargetEndpointAddress(endPointURL);
getNamesCall.setOperationName(
   new QName("ImageService", "getNames"));
getNamesCall.addParameter("extension",
   org.apache.axis.encoding.XMLType.XSD_STRING,
   ParameterMode.IN);
getNamesCall.setReturnType(XMLType.SOAP_ARRAY);
```

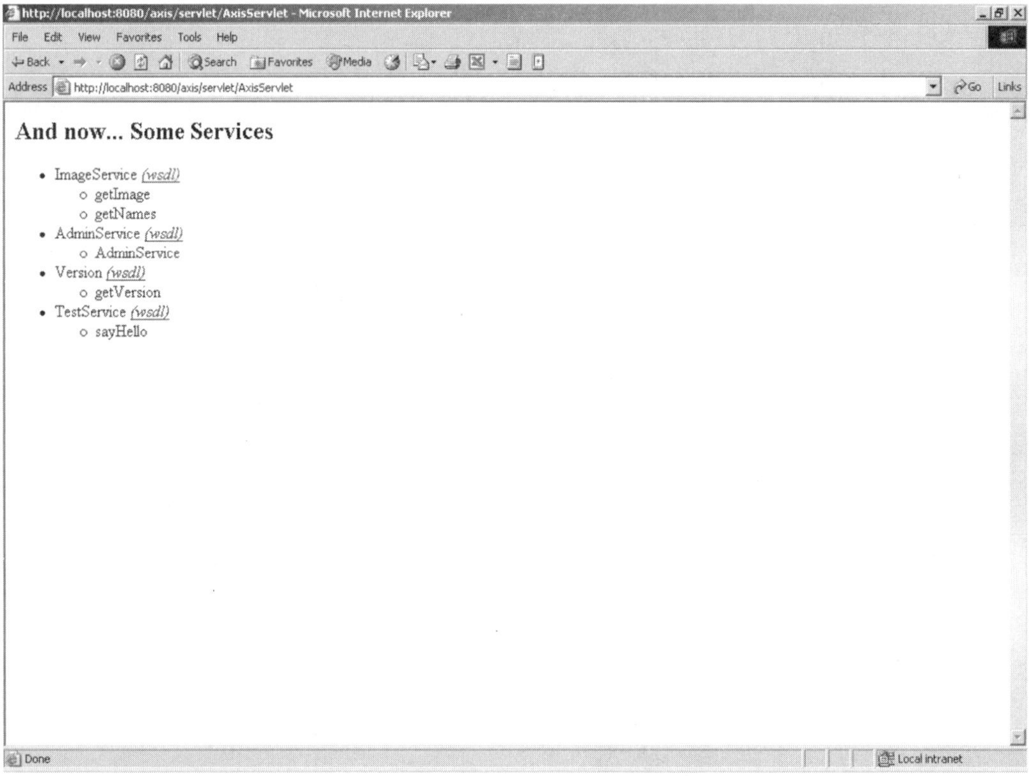

Figure 8.4   Web services deployed on Axis

2. Invoke the call. In this case, the getNames method returns an array of
   String, so we need to cast the invoke method to String[].

```
String[] names = (String[])getNamesCall.invoke(
  new Object[] { ".png" });
```

3. Process the response.

```
if (names == null) {
   System.out.println("The array of names is null");
}
else {
   System.out.println("Image names:");
   for (int i=0; i<names.length; i++)
      System.out.println("  " + names[i]);
}
```

4. Catch exceptions during these calls. Axis will throw an `AxisFault` exception if something goes wrong, so we need to make sure we catch it. In this case, we will just send it to `System.out`.

```
catch (AxisFault fault) {
   System.err.println("Generated fault: ");
   System.out.println("  Fault Code   = " +
     fault.getFaultCode());
   System.out.println("  Fault String = " +
     fault.getFaultString());
}
```

The Ant build file has a target to run this test client, called `RunImageServiceClient`. It appears like this:

```
<target name="RunImageServiceClient" depends="CompileDesktop">
  <java
     classname="com.javaonpdas.client.ImageServiceClient"
     dir="."
     fork="true"
     failonerror="true">
     <classpath>
       <pathelement path="${desktopdest}"/>
       <path refid="axis.path"/>
     </classpath>
     <arg line="${testendpoint}"/>
  </java>
</target>
```

Run the test client by typing ant `RunImageServiceClient` on the command line:

```
C:\JavaOnPDAs>ant RunImageServiceClient
Buildfile: build.xml

Init:

CompileDesktop:

RunImageServiceClient:
     [java] Image names:
     [java]   kookaburra.png
     [java]   kookaburra-bw.png
     [java]   kangaroo-bw.png
     [java]   kangaroo1.png
     [java]   kangaroo2.png
     [java]   kangaroo3.png
```

```
[java] Image returned is kangaroo1.png
[java]   image date is Mon, 04 Nov 2002 21:08:50
[java]   image is 1458 bytes long
```

```
BUILD SUCCESSFUL
Total time: 7 seconds
```

Monitoring HTTP Traffic

Axis comes with a very useful debugging tool, called TcpMon. TcpMon allows you to view the request sent from the client and the response received from the server. The way it works is to create a TCP/IP "tunnel" between a dummy port to which the client is pointed, and the real port on which the server is running. For example, we can tell TcpMon to listen on port 5555 and to connect clients to port 8080 (where Tomcat listens), and to display all traffic going between the two ports, such as our Web service requests and responses.

To start TcpMon, the Ant build file has a target called RunTcpMon. It starts on the port ${test-axis-port}, which is set to 5555. The Ant target looks like this:

```
<target name="RunTcpMon">
  <java
    classname="org.apache.axis.utils.tcpmon"
    dir="."
    fork="true"
    failonerror="true">
    <classpath>
      <path refid="axis.path"/>
    </classpath>
    <arg line="${test-axis-port} localhost ${axis-port}"/>
  </java>
</target>
```

To start it, type ant RunTcpMon on the command line. When it starts, TcpMon looks like the window shown in Figure 8.5.

To tell the ImageServiceClient that we want to connect to port 5555, make sure that the Ant build file has the following value for the testendpoint property:

```
<property name="testendpoint"
value="http://localhost:${test-axis-port}/axis/servlet/AxisServlet"/>
```

When you run the client, you should see TcpMon display the request and response, as shown in Figure 8.6.

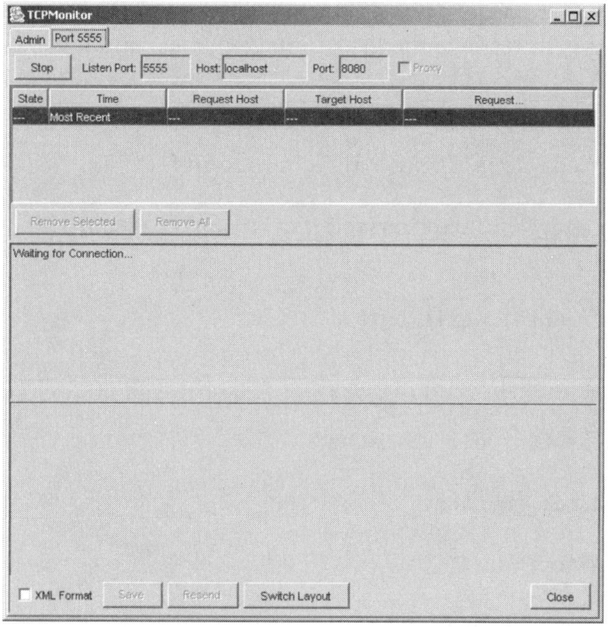

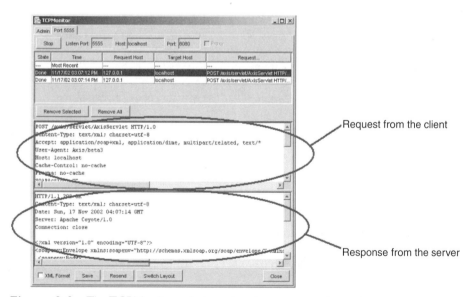

Figure 8.5 The TCPMonitor window

Figure 8.6 The TCPMonitor window showing an example session

The `ImageServiceClient` sends two separate requests to the server. The first is to retrieve the list of image names, and it looks like this:

```
POST /axis/servlet/AxisServlet HTTP/1.0

Content-Type: text/xml; charset=utf-8

Accept: application/soap+xml, application/dime, multipart/related,
text/*

User-Agent: Axis/beta3

Host: localhost

Cache-Control: no-cache

Pragma: no-cache

SOAPAction: ""

Content-Length: 446


<?xml version="1.0" encoding="UTF-8"?>
<soapenv:Envelope xmlns:soapenv="http://schemas.xmlsoap.org/soap/
envelope/" xmlns:xsd="http://www.w3.org/2001/XMLSchema"
xmlns:xsi="http://www.w3.org/2001/XMLSchema-instance">
 <soapenv:Body>
  <ns1:getNames soapenv:encodingStyle="http://schemas.xmlsoap.org/
soap/encoding/" xmlns:ns1="ImageService">
   <extension xsi:type="xsd:string">.png</extension>
  </ns1:getNames>
 </soapenv:Body>
</soapenv:Envelope>
```

And the response looks like this:

```
HTTP/1.1 200 OK

Content-Type: text/xml; charset=utf-8

Date: Sat, 07 Dec 2002 12:21:33 GMT

Server: Apache Coyote/1.0

Connection: close
```

```xml
<?xml version="1.0" encoding="UTF-8"?>
<soapenv:Envelope xmlns:soapenv="http://schemas.xmlsoap.org/soap/
envelope/" xmlns:xsd="http://www.w3.org/2001/XMLSchema"
xmlns:xsi="http://www.w3.org/2001/XMLSchema-instance">
 <soapenv:Body>
  <ns1:getNamesResponse soapenv:encodingStyle="http://
schemas.xmlsoap.org/soap/encoding/" xmlns:ns1="ImageService">
   <getNamesReturn xsi:type="soapenc:Array"
soapenc:arrayType="xsd:string[4]" xmlns:soapenc="http://
schemas.xmlsoap.org/soap/encoding/">
    <item>kookaburra.png</item>
    <item>kookaburra-bw.png</item>
    <item>kangaroo-bw.png</item>
    <item>kangaroo1.png</item>
   </getNamesReturn>
  </ns1:getNamesResponse>
 </soapenv:Body>
</soapenv:Envelope>
```

Undeploying the Web Service

To undeploy the Web service, we again use the Axis administration client. The Ant build file defines a target to undeploy the image service, called UndeployImageService. The target is defined as follows:

```xml
<target name="UndeployImageService">
  <!-- Undeploy the ImageService web service -->
  <java
      classname="org.apache.axis.client.AdminClient"
      dir="."
      fork="true"
      failonerror="true">
      <classpath>
        <pathelement path="${desktopdest}"/>
        <path refid="axis.path"/>
      </classpath>
      <arg line="-l${webserviceadmin}↵
${desktopsrc}\com\javaonpdas\webservices\undeploy-ImageService-↵
AXIS.wsdd"/>
  </java>
</target>
```

Typing the command ant `UndeployImageService` should get the following response:

```
C:\JavaOnPDAs>ant UndeployImageService
Buildfile: build.xml

UndeployImageService:
    [java] - Processing file
.\Desktop\src\com\javaonpdas\webservices\undeploy-
ImageService-AXIS.wsdd
    [java] - <Admin>Done processing</Admin>

BUILD SUCCESSFUL
Total time: 14 seconds
```

To verify that Axis has indeed removed the service, point your browser back to the main Axis page at `http://127.0.0.1:8080/axis/index.html` and click on the `View` link. The `ImageService` should not be listed as a service that Axis knows about. Note that the `undeploy` command merely removes the Web service definition from Axis—it does not remove the JAR file we put in the webapp `lib` directory.

The ImageViewer Client Application

Now that we have tested the ImageService with a desktop client, we will write a PDA client. We will start with a Palm version, and then move on to a PocketPC version. In each case the client will allow the user to

- View a list of names of images available on the server.
- View a list of names of images available on the client.
- Select an image name and view the image.
- Store a remote image on the client.

Before we start writing the Palm version of the `ImageViewer` application, we will explore some options for accessing a Web service from the Palm.

Web Service Access from a Palm Device

Calling a Web Service Directly

In this option, the Palm calls the Web service directly as shown in Figure 8.7.

We will need a SOAP client for J2ME. There are several popular clients available, such as kSOAP (`http://www.ksoap.org`) and Wingfoot (`http://`

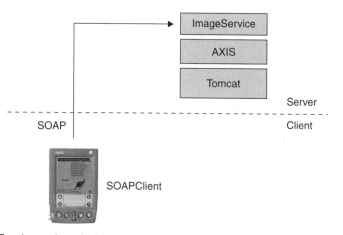

Figure 8.7 Accessing a Web service directly from the Palm device

www.wingfoot.com). For this client, we will choose the Wingfoot SOAP client. It also has a J2SE version, which we will use for the PocketPC client.

Download the latest Wingfoot SOAP client from http://www.wingfoot.com/. Note that you will need to register by providing your email address and your name. The examples in this book use Wingfoot 1.03.

Unzip the downloaded ZIP file into a convenient location. The ZIP will contain two JAR files: one for J2ME named kvmwsoap_1.03.jar and the other for J2SE named j2sewsoap_1.03.jar. Copy the J2ME JAR to the ${palm-base}\lib directory.

In the example application, com.javaonpdas.webservices.clients.wingfoot. SOAPClient, the application has two buttons: one to retrieve the names and the other to retrieve the image, specified by a hard-coded name.

When the "Get Names" button is pressed, we create an Envelope object and use it to create a Call object. The Call object represents the service invocation we want to make, so we need to specify the name of the service to invoke and the service's method name.

```
Envelope requestEnvelope = new Envelope();
requestEnvelope.setBody("extension", ".png");
Call call = new Call(requestEnvelope);
call.setMethodName("getNames");
call.setTargetObjectURI("ImageService");
```

Next we set up the transport by telling it the SOAP endpoint. Note that the hostname in the URL is not localhost, as the Palm will interpret that as meaning the Palm device rather than the machine where the Web service resides.

```
HTTPTransport transport =
  new HTTPTransport("http://192.168.0.1:8080/axis/servlet/|↵
AxisServlet", null);
transport.getResponse(true);
```

The transport object is used to invoke the call, and the result is assigned to an Envelope object.

```
Envelope responseEnvelope = call.invoke(transport);
```

Then the envelope is queried to process its contents. If an error occurred, isFaultGenerated will return true. In this case we need to retrieve the fault from the envelope and, in this case, display it on the screen. Otherwise, the response to the Web service invocation is in the 0th parameter, represented as an array of Object. These are the names of the images available on the server, so we insert them at the end of the text field and add a new line character.

```
if (responseEnvelope != null) {
   if (responseEnvelope.isFaultGenerated()) {
      Fault f = responseEnvelope.getFault();
      textField.insert("Error: " + f.getFaultString(),
      textField.size());
   }
   else {
      textField.setString(null);
      Object[] parameter =
        (Object[])responseEnvelope.getParameter(0);
      for (int i=0; i<parameter.length; i++)
         textField.insert(parameter[i] + "\n",
           textField.size());
   }
}
```

The code to handle the "Get Image" button press is similar but there are some important extensions. The first difference is in the set up of the envelope, where we set the parameter for the method we want to call.

```
Envelope requestEnvelope = new Envelope();
requestEnvelope.setBody("name", "kangaroo1.png");
```

When we set up the Call object, there are some other differences compared to the "Get Names" case above. In this case, the Web service method we want to invoke returns an object we defined, rather than a standard object (i.e., String) as was the case in "Get Names." The ImageService's getImage method returns an ImageValue, so we need to specify that in setting up the Call object using a `TypeMappingRegistry`. The `TypeMappingRegistry` tells the SOAP client how to deal with the `ImageValue` type returned by the `getImage` method.

```
Call call = new Call(requestEnvelope);
call.setMethodName("getImage");
call.setTargetObjectURI("ImageService");
TypeMappingRegistry registry =
  new TypeMappingRegistry();
registry.mapTypes("urn:BeanService", "ImageValue",
  new ImageValue().getClass(),
  new BeanSerializer().getClass(),
  new BeanSerializer().getClass());
call.setMappingRegistry(registry);
```

The `registry.mapTypes` method creates a new entry in the registry that maps between the custom SOAP type `ImageValue` in the namespace `urn:BeanService` and the bean serializer and deserializer class `ImageValue`. The client then knows that the `ImageValue` class is used to serialize and deserialize the type `ImageValue`.

The transport is set up as before.

```
HTTPTransport transport = new HTTPTransport("http://↵
192.168.0.1:8080/axis/servlet/AxisServlet", null);
transport.getResponse(true);
```

And the service is invoked.

```
Envelope responseEnvelope = call.invoke(transport);
```

Next we process the response in a similar way to the "Get Names" case, except this time we are expecting an `ImageValue` instance.

```
ImageValue imageValue = (ImageValue)responseEnvelope.getParameter(0);
```

Now that we have the instance of `ImageValue`, containing the image in encoded form as received from the server, we need to decode the Base64-encoded string back into an image. The Wingfoot SOAP client JAR includes a Base64 encoder and decoder, so we will use that.

To decode the encoded string, we use the `String` constructor of the class `Base64`, and then the getBytes method to retrieve the byte array. The `Image` class has a static method `createImage` that takes a byte array, which we use to create an immutable image for the `ImageItem` on the main screen.

```
Base64 encodedImage =
  new Base64(imageValue.getEncodedImage());
```

```
imageItem.setImage(Image.createImage(
  encodedImage.getBytes(), 0,
  encodedImage.getBytes().length));
```

To run the application, type ant SOAPClient. The emulator will start and the screen will look like the screen in Figure 8.8.

Pressing the "Get Names" button will result in the invocation of the ImageService Web service, and the Palm will display on the screen the names of images on the server, as shown in Figure 8.9.

Pressing the "Get Image" button will cause the getImage method of the ImageService service to be invoked, and the image kangaroo1.png is displayed on the screen, similar to Figure 8.10.

Using a Proxy with HTTP to Access the Web Service

Having a SOAP client on the Palm device means that there is less space for your application, and valuable processing resources are used to generate the SOAP request and parse the response. Often in constrained environments, we need to find a way to off-load processing from the device if at all possible. In this section, we look at one such alternative. Off-loading processing from the

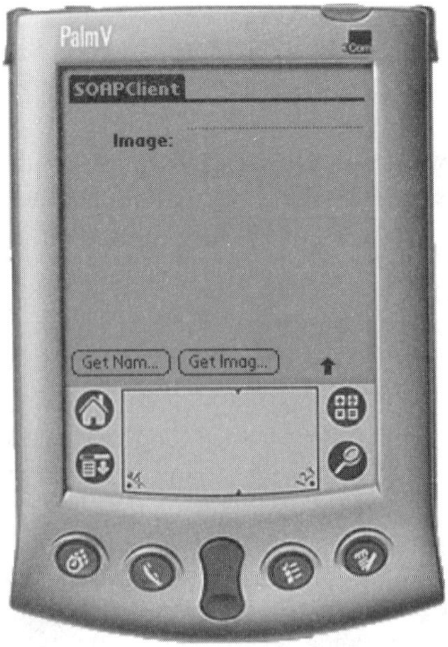

Figure 8.8   The SOAPClient window

Figure 8.9 Image names returned by the Web service

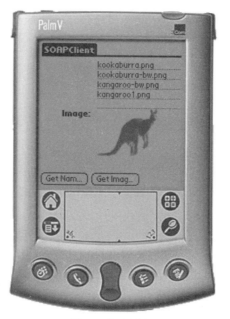

Figure 8.10 An image returned from the Web service

device means that we need to do some more processing on the server side. The server side is relatively unconstrained in processing resources, so it makes sense to do more there than on the constrained mobile device. We need some processing to be done on the server on behalf of the Palm device. The processing interacts with the Web service, and the Web service is unchanged. The results of this processing are sent to the device in a form that it can process with a minimum of effort. The logic to perform this processing is called a proxy.

One approach to building a proxy to interact with the ImageService on the Palm's behalf is to use a servlet. A servlet provides classes that make it very easy to create server-side logic accessed with HTTP as shown in Figure 8.11.

The Palm will invoke the servlet using HTTP GET and a URL, and retrieve the information as text in a Web page. The URL will embed some parameters that form the protocol between the Palm and the proxy. The first parameter is the service endpoint (the name is "service-end-point"), the value of which is a URL that tells the proxy where to find the ImageService Web service. The second parameter named "action" tells the proxy which ImageService method to invoke. The values will be "getNames" and "getImage." If the action is "getImage," another parameter named "name" has the value of the image to retrieve.

The first thing is to create a class that extends HttpServlet:

```
public class ImageServiceProxy extends HttpServlet {

}
```

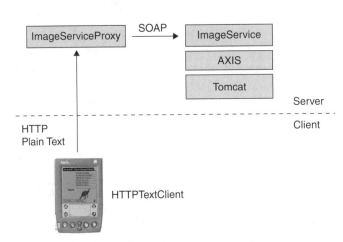

Figure 8.11   Accessing the Web service via a server-side proxy

Next we will implement the doGet method. This method gets the values of the parameters and invokes the ImageService methods accordingly. It then writes the response to the servlet's output stream.

```java
public void doGet(HttpServletRequest request,
    HttpServletResponse response) throws IOException,
    ServletException {
  URL endPointURL = new URL(request.getParameter("service-end-point"));
  String action = request.getParameter("action");
  if (action.equalsIgnoreCase("getNames")) {
     String[] names = getNames(endPointURL);
     response.setContentType("text/plain");
     PrintWriter out = response.getWriter();
     if (names != null) {
        for (int i=0; i<names.length; i++)
           out.println(names[i]);
     }
  }
  else if (action.equalsIgnoreCase("getImage")) {
     String name = request.getParameter("name");
     ImageValue imageValue = getImage(endPointURL, name);
     if (imageValue == null) {
        System.out.println("imageValue is null");
     }
     else {
        response.setContentType("text/plain");
        StringBuffer buffer = new StringBuffer();
        buffer.append(""+imageValue.getDate()+"\n");
        buffer.append(imageValue.getEncodedImage()+"\n");
        response.setContentLength(buffer.length());
        PrintWriter out = response.getWriter();
        out.println(buffer.toString());
     }
  }
  else {
     // action not recognised
  }
}
```

The doGet method makes use of some helper methods, for accessing the ImageService Web service. The purpose of these methods is to separate the Web service access from the main servlet logic, as they are logically distinct.

```java
private String[] getNames(URL endPointURL) {
   String[] names = null;
   try {
```

```java
      Service service = new Service();
      Call call = (Call)service.createCall();
      call.setTargetEndpointAddress(endPointURL);
      call.setOperationName(new QName("ImageService", "getNames"));
      names = (String[])call.invoke(new Object[] {});
    }
    catch (AxisFault fault) {
      System.err.println("Generated fault: ");
      System.out.println("  Fault Code   = " + fault.getFaultCode());
      System.out.println("  Fault String = " + fault.getFaultString());
    }
    catch (Exception e) {
      System.out.println(e.toString());
    }
    return names;
  }

  private ImageValue getImage(URL endPointURL, String name) {
    ImageValue imageValue = null;
    try {
      // Set up the SOAP Service Object
      Service service = new Service();
      Call call = (Call)service.createCall();
      call.setTargetEndpointAddress(endPointURL);
      call.setOperationName(new QName("ImageService", "getImage"));
      call.addParameter("name",
        org.apache.axis.encoding.XMLType.XSD_STRING,
        ParameterMode.IN);
      QName qn = new QName("urn:BeanService", "ImageValue");
      call.registerTypeMapping(ImageValue.class, qn,
        new BeanSerializerFactory(ImageValue.class, qn),
        new BeanDeserializerFactory(ImageValue.class, qn));
      call.setReturnType(qn);

      imageValue = (ImageValue)call.invoke(new Object[] { name });
    }
    catch (AxisFault fault) {
      System.err.println("Generated fault: ");
      System.out.println("  Fault Code   = " + fault.getFaultCode());
      System.out.println("  Fault String = " + fault.getFaultString());
    }
    catch (Exception e) {
      System.out.println(e.toString());
    }
    return imageValue;
  }
```

To deploy the servlet to run on Tomcat, we will need to set up a new Web application. We will call the Web application "javaonpdas," and so we need to create a new directory under ${tomcat-base}\webapps called javaonpdas. In the javaonpdas directory, we need a WEB-INF directory, which in turn should contain a lib directory for the JAR files for the Web application.

In the directory ${tomcat-base}\webapps\javaonpdas\WEB-INF we need to put a web.xml file that describes the new Web application. The web.xml file describes the servlet class that implements the Web application, as well as the URL pattern to be used to access the servlet. The servlet section describes this. Normally we do not want the servlet accessed with a long-winded URL that includes the fully qualified class name—we can use a shorthand name instead. The servlet-mapping section sets this up.

```xml
<?xml version="1.0" encoding="ISO-8859-1"?>

<!DOCTYPE web-app
    PUBLIC "-//Sun Microsystems, Inc.//DTD Web Application 2.2//EN"
    "http://java.sun.com/j2ee/dtds/web-app_2.2.dtd">

<web-app>
  <servlet>
    <servlet-name>ImageServiceProxy</servlet-name>
    <display-name>ImageServiceProxy</display-name>
    <servlet-class>
        com.javaonpdas.proxy.ImageServiceProxy
    </servlet-class>
  </servlet>

  <servlet-mapping>
    <servlet-name>ImageServiceProxy</servlet-name>
    <url-pattern>/servlet/ImageServiceProxy</url-pattern>
  </servlet-mapping>

</web-app>
```

With these mappings in place, we can access the new servlet with the following URL:

```
http://192.168.0.1:8080/javaonpdas/servlet/ImageServiceProxy
```

Because our Web application is an Axis SOAP client, we will copy the Axis client JARs into the ${tomcat-base}\webapps\javaonpdas\WEB-INF\lib directory. The JARs are

```
axis.jar
jaxrpc.jar
axis-ant.jar
commons-discovery.jar
commons-logging.jar
log4j-1.2.4.jar
saaj.jar
wsdl4j.jar
```

The `ImageServiceProxy` class is compiled and deployed as part of the `CompileDesktop` target in the Ant build file. The resultant JAR `javaonpdas-desktop.jar` is also copied to the `${tomcat-base}\webapps\javaonpdas\WEB-INF\lib` directory.

Once the set up of the new Web application is complete, we can test it. Restart Tomcat and use a browser to access the following URL:

```
http://192.168.0.1:8080/javaonpdas/servlet/↵
ImageServiceProxy?service-end-point=http://localhost:8080/axis/↵
servlet/AxisServlet&action=getNames
```

This URL is invoking the new `ImageServiceProxy` servlet, telling it the Web service endpoint to use (`http://localhost:8080/axis/servlet/AxisServlet`), and the action to perform (`action=getNames`).

Because the proxy accepts a URL and writes the result in plain text, we can see the result in the Web page in Figure 8.12.

Similarly, we can use the following URL to retrieve the Base64-encoded image kookaburra.png:

```
http://192.168.0.1:8080/javaonpdas/servlet/↵
ImageServiceProxy?service-end-point=http://localhost:8080/axis/↵
servlet/AxisServlet&action=getImage&name=kookaburra.png
```

The first line in Figure 8.13 is the long integer corresponding to the image's last modified date, and the second line in the Base64-encoded string of the image itself.

To create a Palm client that accesses the proxy rather than the Web service directly, we will modify `SOAPClient` and create a new MIDlet called HTTPTextClient. This MIDlet is similar except for the way the `getNames` and `getImage` commands are handled.

The first step is to set up the HTTP connection by opening the input stream.

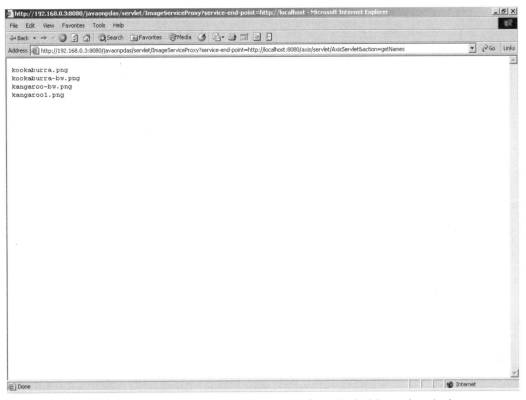

Figure 8.12 Using a browser to return image names from the Web service via the proxy

```
HttpConnection connection = null;
InputStream is = null;
String url = "http://192.168.0.1:8080/javaonpdas/servlet/↵
ImageServiceProxy?service-end-point=http://localhost:8080/axis/↵
servlet/AxisServlet&action=getNames";
try {
    connection = (HttpConnection)Connector.open(url);
    connection.setRequestMethod(HttpConnection.GET);
    is = connection.openInputStream();
    int contentLength = (int)connection.getLength();
```

Assuming the content length is not zero, we create a byte array to accommodate the content, and read from the input stream.

```
byte[] byteArray = new byte[contentLength];
is.read(byteArray);
```

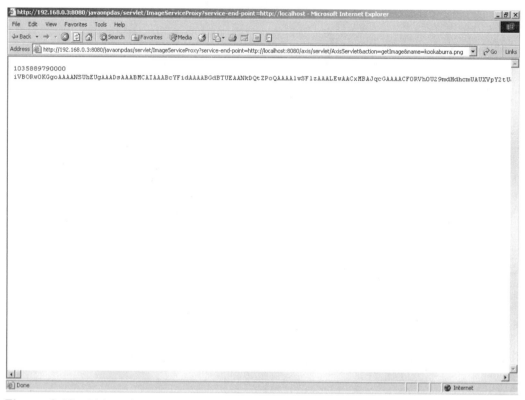

Figure 8.13   Using a browser to retrieve the Base64 representation of an image

Next we parse the byte array looking for '\n' characters, indicating the end of an image file name. For each file name, we add the string to the text field.

```
StringBuffer buffer = new StringBuffer();
textField.setString(null);
for (int i=0; i<byteArray.length; i++) {
    if (byteArray[i] == (byte)'\n') {
        textField.insert(buffer.toString() + "\n", textField.size());
        buffer.setLength(0);
    }
    else if (byteArray[i] == (byte)'\r') {
    }
    else {
        buffer.append((char)byteArray[i]);
    }
}
```

Figure 8.14 Accessing the Web service via the HTTP text proxy

Running ant `HTTPTextClient` compiles the application and starts the emulator. Pressing the "Get Names" button will result in the image file names being displayed as before and as shown in Figure 8.14, except that this time the Palm is communicating with the Web service proxy, rather than the Web service itself.

Using a Proxy with Data Streams to Access the Web Service

An alternative to using HTTP and plain text is to open a stream over the HTTP socket connection between the client and the proxy. A proxy that demonstrates this approach is `ImageServiceStreamProxy`, as shown in Figure 8.15.

The code in `ImageServiceStreamProxy` differs from `ImageServiceProxy` mainly in the way that the information is sent back to the client; the same protocol as that used in `ImageServiceProxy` is used for embedding the request in the URL.

The `doGet` method in `ImageServiceStreamProxy` calls the helper methods to access the Web service as before, but instead of writing the response to a `PrintWriter`, it opens a `DataOutputStream` and writes the response to it.

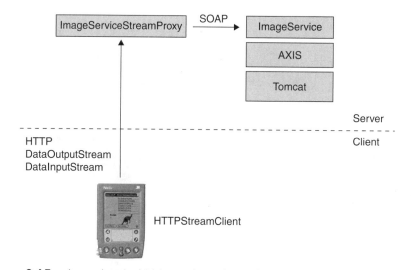

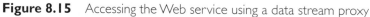

Figure 8.15　Accessing the Web service using a data stream proxy

```
if (action.equalsIgnoreCase("getNames")) {
   String[] names = getNames(endPointURL);
   DataOutputStream dos = null;
   try {
      dos = new DataOutputStream(response.getOutputStream());
      if (names != null) {
         dos.writeInt(names.length);
         for (int i=0; i<names.length; i++)
            dos.writeUTF(names[i]);
      }
      else
         dos.writeInt(0);
   }
   catch (Exception e) {
      System.out.println(e.toString());
   }
   finally {
      try { if (dos != null) dos.close(); } catch (Exception e) {}
   }
}
```

In the "getNames" case, the helper method getNames() is called to retrieve the file names as before. Then a DataOutputStream is opened on the response's output stream. The first thing to write to the DataOutputStream is the number of names in the list, so that the client knows how many to expect. Then we write the file names using writeUTF().

In the "getImage" case, we can decode the image from the Base64 string into an array of bytes and write the byte array to the DataOutputStream. This saves the client from decoding the string, which is consistent with our objective of doing as much work as possible on the server.

```
else if (action.equalsIgnoreCase("getImage")) {
   String name = request.getParameter("name");
   ImageValue imageValue = getImage(endPointURL, name);
   if (imageValue == null) {
     System.out.println("imageValue is null");
   }
   else {
      byte[] byteArray = org.apache.axis.encoding.Base64.decode(
        imageValue.getEncodedImage());
      System.out.println("image length="+byteArray.length);
      response.setContentLength(byteArray.length);
      DataOutputStream dos = null;
      try {
         dos = new DataOutputStream(response.getOutputStream());
         dos.write(byteArray, 0, byteArray.length);
      }
      catch (Exception e) {
         System.out.println(e.toString());
      }
      finally {
         try { if (dos != null) dos.close(); } catch (Exception e) {}
      }
   }
}
```

To use this new proxy based on streams, we need to modify the client to use streams as well. The client is called HTTPStreamClient. The client makes the request in the same way as before but retrieves the result by opening a DataInputStream on the HTTP connection.

```
if (c == getNamesCommand) {
   HttpConnection connection = null;
   DataInputStream dis = null;
   String url = "http://192.168.0.1:8080/javaonpdas/servlet/↵
ImageServiceStreamProxy?service-end-point=http://localhost:8080/↵
axis/servlet/AxisServlet&action=getNames";
   try {
       connection = (HttpConnection)Connector.open(url);
       connection.setRequestMethod(HttpConnection.GET);
```

```
         dis = connection.openDataInputStream();
         int numberOfNames = dis.readInt();
         textField.setString(null);
         for (int i=0; i<numberOfNames; i++) {
            String name = dis.readUTF();
            textField.insert(name + "\n", textField.size());
         }
      }
   }
   catch (Exception e) {
      textField.insert("Error:" + e.toString() + "\n", textField.size());
   }
   finally {
      try {
         if (connection != null) connection.close();
         if (dis != null) dis.close();
      } catch (Exception e) {}
   }
}
```

The first thing to read from the DataInputStream is the number of file names sent by the proxy. Then we loop that number of times, reading the strings from the input stream and displaying them on the text field.

In the case of "Get Image," again we set up a DataInputStream on the HTTP connection, read the array of bytes from the stream, and create an image from the array. Recall that the Base64 string was decoded on the server by the proxy.

```
else if (c == getImageCommand) {
   HttpConnection connection = null;
   DataInputStream dis = null;
   String url = "http://192.168.0.1:8080/javaonpdas/servlet/↵
ImageServiceStreamProxy?service-end-point=http://localhost:8080/↵
axis/servlet/AxisServlet&action=getImage&name=Kangaroo.png";
   try {
      connection = (HttpConnection)Connector.open(url);
      connection.setRequestMethod(HttpConnection.GET);
      int contentLength = (int)connection.getLength();
      if (contentLength>0) {
         dis = connection.openDataInputStream();
         byte[] imageByteArray = new byte[contentLength];
         int ch = 0;
         for (int i=0; i<contentLength; i++) {
            if ((ch = dis.read()) != -1) {
               imageByteArray[i] = (byte)ch;
            }
            else {
```

```
                    textField.insert("Error: encountered EOF\n",
                                textField.size());
            }
        }
        imageItem.setImage(Image.createImage(imageByteArray,
                            0, imageByteArray.length));
    }
}
catch (Throwable t) {
    textField.insert("Error:" + t.toString() + "\n",
                    textField.size());
    t.printStackTrace();
}
finally {
    try {
        if (dis != null) dis.close();
        if (connection != null) connection.close();
    } catch (Exception e) {}
}
}
```

Comparing Performance

The three access methods were tested on a Palm IIIx with a direct serial connection to a PC, and their performance is compared in Table 8.2.

In the next section, we will compare these access methods.

Summary of Web Service Access Options

The following comparison describes the advantages of each option over the other options. The disadvantages are of each option are compared to the other options. The reason for using a particular option is also given.

Table 8.2 Comparing Performance of Web Service Access Methods

	SOAP	HTTPText	HTTPStream
Size of PRC (bytes)	80,800	12,925	9,509
Free memory at runtime (bytes)	61,864	62,576	62,576
Memory used (bytes)	288	2,752	2,444
Time to request and retrieve image (ms)	28,090	9,010	7,420

SOAP

Advantages

- No client-specific proxy is required on the server.

Disadvantages

- SOAP on the client uses precious memory and processing power.
- Slower and uses more memory compared to the proxy methods.

HTTP Text

Advantages

- Simple protocol to exchange information with the client.
- The server handles the overhead of the SOAP connection.

Disadvantages

- Requires a client-specific proxy on the server.

HTTPStream

Advantages

- Simple protocol to exchange information with the client.
- Can decode the Base64 string on the server, thus making less work for the client.
- The server handles the overhead of the SOAP connection.
- Uses a binary connection, meaning there is no need to detect string boundaries.
- The fastest of the three access methods compared, and uses the least memory.

Disadvantages

- Requires a client-specific proxy on the server.

Palm ImageViewer

Because the HTTP stream method uses the least memory and is the fastest end-to-end, we will use this method for the Palm version of ImageViewer.

The ImageViewer constructor sets up the application display. We will use a ChoiceGroup for selecting the image to display, another ChoiceGroup for selecting locally or remotely stored images, an ImageItem to display the image, a Command for saving remote images to local storage, and a Command for exiting the application.

Here is the constructor code:

```
public ImageViewer() {
    // populate the list with local names
    String[] names = getNames(true);
    if (names == null)
      nameChoice =
        new ChoiceGroup("Names", ChoiceGroup.EXCLUSIVE, NAMES, null);
    else
      nameChoice =
        new ChoiceGroup("Names", ChoiceGroup.EXCLUSIVE, names, null);
    // add the items to the form
    mainForm.append(nameChoice);
    mainForm.append(locationChoice);
    mainForm.append(imageItem);
    mainForm.addCommand(saveCommand);
    mainForm.addCommand(exitCommand);
    mainForm.setCommandListener(this);
    mainForm.setItemStateListener(this);
}
```

Note that the `ImageViewer` class implements two interfaces: the `CommandListener` interface and the `ItemStateListener` interface.

```
public class ImageViewer extends MIDlet
implements CommandListener, ItemStateListener
```

This is because we need to listen for `Command` selections, and state changes and name selections in the `ChoiceGroups`.

The screen looks like Figure 8.16 on starting the application.

Selecting the Location `ChoiceGroup` causes the `itemStateChanged` method to be called. Making a choice of location results in the `Names` list being populated with image names according to the Location selection. Selecting an image name results in the image being displayed on the screen.

```
public void itemStateChanged(Item item) {
    Runtime.getRuntime().gc();
    try {
      String location = locationChoice.getString(
                          locationChoice.getSelectedIndex());
      System.out.println("location: " + location);
      imageItem.setLabel("Please wait...");
      if (item == locationChoice) {
          String[] names = getNames(location.equals("Local"));
          System.out.println("there are " + names.length + " names");
          int namesInList = nameChoice.size();
```

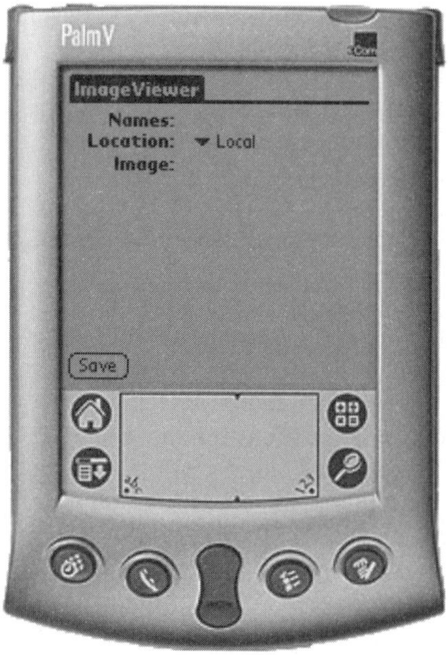

Figure 8.16   The Palm OS version of ImageViewer

```
        for (int i=0; i<namesInList; i++)
            nameChoice.delete(0);
        for (int i=0; i<names.length; i++)
            nameChoice.append(names[i], null);
        imageItem.setImage(Image.createImage(
            Image.createImage(10,10)));
    }
    else if (item == nameChoice) {
        String name =
            nameChoice.getString(nameChoice.getSelectedIndex());
        imageItem.setImage(Image.createImage(
            Image.createImage(10,10)));
        Image image = getImage(name, location.equals("Local"));
        imageItem.setImage(image);
    }
    imageItem.setLabel("Image");
}
catch (Exception e) {
    System.out.println("Error: " + e.toString());
}
}
```

Images are stored on the client in a RecordStore. The image names are retrieved from the RecordStore as follows:

```
store = RecordStore.openRecordStore(recordStoreName, true);
RecordEnumeration re = store.enumerateRecords(null, null, false);
names = new String[re.numRecords()];
int i=0;
while(re.hasNextElement()) {
   ByteArrayInputStream bis = new ByteArrayInputStream(re.nextRecord());
   dis = new DataInputStream(bis);
   names[i++] = dis.readUTF();
}
store.closeRecordStore();
```

When a local image name is selected, the image is retrieved from the RecordStore as follows:

```
RecordStore store = null;
try {
   store = RecordStore.openRecordStore(recordStoreName, true);
   RecordEnumeration re =
      store.enumerateRecords(null, null, false);
   while(re.hasNextElement()) {
      ByteArrayInputStream bis =
         new ByteArrayInputStream(re.nextRecord());
      dis = new DataInputStream(bis);
      if (dis.readUTF().equals(name)) {
         int imageSize = dis.readInt();
         imageByteArray = new byte[imageSize];
         dis.readFully(imageByteArray);
         image = Image.createImage(imageByteArray,
            0, imageByteArray.length);
      }
   }
   store.closeRecordStore();
}
catch (Exception e) {
   System.out.println("Error:" + e.toString());
}
finally {
   try {
      if (store != null) store.closeRecordStore();
      if (dis != null) dis.close();
   } catch (Exception e) {}
}
```

To retrieve the image names from the server, the following code should look familiar from the previous examples:

```
String url = "http://192.168.0.1:8080/javaonpdas/servlet/↵
ImageServiceStreamProxy?service-end-point=http://localhost:8080/↵
axis/servlet/AxisServlet&action=getNames";
connection = (HttpConnection)Connector.open(url);
connection.setRequestMethod(HttpConnection.GET);
dis = connection.openDataInputStream();
int numberOfNames = dis.readInt();
names = new String[numberOfNames];
for (int i=0; i<numberOfNames; i++) {
    names[i] = dis.readUTF();
}
```

Retrieving the image from the server is the same technique we used in the HTTPStreamClient:

```
HttpConnection connection = null;
String url = "http://192.168.0.1:8080/javaonpdas/servlet/↵
ImageServiceStreamProxy?service-end-point=http://localhost:8080/↵
axis/servlet/AxisServlet&action=getImage&name="+name;
try {
    connection = (HttpConnection)Connector.open(url);
    connection.setRequestMethod(HttpConnection.GET);
    int contentLength = (int)connection.getLength();
    if (contentLength>0) {
        dis = connection.openDataInputStream();
        imageByteArray = new byte[contentLength];
        int ch = 0;
        for (int i=0; i<contentLength; i++) {
            if ((ch = dis.read()) != -1) {
                imageByteArray[i] = (byte)ch;
            }
            else {
                System.out.println("Error: encountered EOF");
            }
        }
        image = Image.createImage(imageByteArray, 0,
                                  imageByteArray.length);
    }
}
catch (Throwable t) {
    System.out.println("Error:" + t.toString());
    t.printStackTrace();
}
```

```
finally {
   try {
      if (dis != null) dis.close();
      if (connection != null) connection.close();
   } catch (Exception e) {}
}
```

Saving an image is only possible if it is remote. In this case, we take the image array already retrieved to display the image and store it in the record store. If the image name already exists in the record store, the stored image is replaced.

First, we open the record store and create a byte array that stores the record store element:

```
store = RecordStore.openRecordStore(recordStoreName, true);
System.out.println("size in bytes (before): "+store.getSize());
// create the new record byte array
ByteArrayOutputStream bos = new ByteArrayOutputStream();
dos = new DataOutputStream(bos);
String name = nameChoice.getString(nameChoice.getSelectedIndex());
dos.writeUTF(name);
dos.writeInt(imageByteArray.length);
dos.write(imageByteArray, 0, imageByteArray.length);
byte[] ba = bos.toByteArray();
```

Then we look for the name in the record store, and update the stored image if the name is already there.

```
RecordEnumeration re = store.enumerateRecords(null, null, false);
System.out.println("looking for " + name + " in " +
   re.numRecords() + " records");
boolean found = false;
int recordID = 1;
while(re.hasNextElement()) {
   ByteArrayInputStream bis =
      new ByteArrayInputStream(re.nextRecord());
   System.out.println("looking at record "+recordID);
   dis = new DataInputStream(bis);
   if (dis.readUTF().equals(name)) {
      System.out.println(name + " found match - updating");
      store.setRecord(recordID, ba, 0, ba.length);
      found = true;
      break;
   }
   else
      System.out.println("no match");
      recordID++;
}
```

If the image name is not found, the image is added and the record store is closed:

```
if (!found) {
    System.out.print(name + " not found - adding " + ba.length);
    int addedID = store.addRecord(ba, 0, ba.length);
    System.out.println(" ID = " + addedID);
}
System.out.println("size in bytes (after): "+store.getSize());
store.closeRecordStore();
```

The full source code for the Palm version of ImageViewer is located in C:\JavaOnPDAs\Palm\src\com\javaonpdas\webservices\clients\custom\ ImageViewer.java.

PocketPC Version

Because the PocketPC is far less constrained in terms of memory and processing capability, a direct SOAP connection to the Web service makes more sense than using the proxy that proved best for a Palm OS implementation. The PocketPC application com.javaonpdas.webservices.clients.wingfoot. ImageViewer takes this approach.

The constructor sets up the Frame. As before, we have a way to select between local and remote, a selection of image names, a button for saving remote images locally, and a component to display the selected image. In the PocketPC case, we will use a radio button for the local/remote selection, and a list box for the image names.

```
public ImageViewer(String title) {
    super(title);
    // handle frame closing events
    addWindowListener(new WindowAdapter() {
        public void windowClosing(WindowEvent e) {
            System.exit(0);
        }
    } );
    // add components
    setLayout(new GridLayout(2,1));
    Panel topPanel = new Panel();
    CheckboxGroup checkBoxGroup = new CheckboxGroup();
    localCheckbox = new Checkbox("Local", checkBoxGroup, true);
    remoteCheckbox = new Checkbox("Remote", checkBoxGroup, false);
    localCheckbox.addItemListener(this);
    remoteCheckbox.addItemListener(this);
```

```
        topPanel.add(localCheckbox);
        topPanel.add(remoteCheckbox);
        saveButton = new Button("Save");
        saveButton.setEnabled(false);
        topPanel.add(saveButton);
        saveButton.addActionListener(this);
        list = new List(4);
        list.addItemListener(this);
        topPanel.add(list);
        add(topPanel);
        imageCanvas = new ImageCanvas();
        add(imageCanvas);
        String[] names = getNames(true);
        if (names != null)
            for (int i=0; i<names.length; i++)
                list.add(names[i]);
}
```

Note that the Save button is disabled when the Local radio button is selected, as it is only possible to save remote images.

The component used for displaying the image is a separate class called ImageCanvas. ImageCanvas is a subclass of Canvas, and separates the job of setting the image and repainting away from the ImageViewer class.

```
package com.javaonpdas.webservices.clients.wingfoot;

import java.awt.Canvas;
import java.awt.Image;
import java.awt.Graphics;
import java.awt.Dimension;

public class ImageCanvas extends Canvas {
    private Image image = null;

    public ImageCanvas() {
        super();
    }

    public void setImage(Image image) {
        this.image = image;
    }

    public Image getImage() {
        return this.image;
    }
```

```
        public void update(Graphics g) {
          paint(g);
        }

        public void paint(Graphics g) {
          if (image != null) {
            Dimension size = getSize();
            g.clearRect(0, 0, size.width, size.height);
            g.drawImage(image, 0, 0, this);
          }
        }
      }
```

There are three events in which we are interested: when the Save button is pressed (triggering an ActionEvent), when the user makes a change in selection between Local and Remote, and when an image name is selected (both of which trigger an ItemEvent).

The ItemEvent is handled by the itemStateChanged method:

```
public void itemStateChanged(ItemEvent evt) {
    if (evt.getItemSelectable().getClass() ==
        new Checkbox().getClass()) {
        local = localCheckbox.getState();
        if (local) saveButton.setEnabled(false);
        else saveButton.setEnabled(true);
        String[] names = getNames(local);
        list.removeAll();
        if (names != null)
            for (int i=0; i<names.length; i++)
                list.add(names[i]);
    }
    else {
        String name = list.getSelectedItem();
        Image image = getImage(name, local);
        imageCanvas.setImage(image);
        imageCanvas.update(imageCanvas.getGraphics());
    }
}
```

If the ItemEvent corresponds to the Local/Remote radio button, we get the image names either stored locally or remotely, depending on the state of the Local button. If the button is set to Local, the Save button is disabled.

If the ItemEvent corresponds to the list of image names, we find the current selection and get the image of that name, and display it on the ImageCanvas.

The ActionEvent is handled by the actionPerformed method:

```
public void actionPerformed(ActionEvent evt) {
    String cmd = evt.getActionCommand();
    if (cmd.startsWith("Save")) {
        Image image = imageCanvas.getImage();
        String name = list.getSelectedItem();
        FileOutputStream ostream = null;
        try {
            ostream = new FileOutputStream(LOCAL_DIRECTORY + "\\" + name);
            ostream.write(imageByteArray);
            ostream.close();
        }
        catch (Exception e) {
            System.out.println("Error:" + e);
        }
        finally {
            try {
                if (ostream != null) ostream.close();
            } catch (Exception e) {}
        }
    }
}
```

If the Save button is pressed, the current image byte array is written to a file in the local image directory using `FileOutputStream`.

The names are retrieved by the `getNames` method, which takes a `Boolean` parameter to indicate whether to retrieve the names from the local or remote repository. In the local case:

```
FilenameFilter filter = new FilenameFilter() {
    public boolean accept(File dir, String name) {
        return name.endsWith(".jpeg");
    }
};
File dir = new File(LOCAL_DIRECTORY);
files = dir.list(filter);
```

Note that we are only interested in JPEG images, where in the Palm Image-Viewer we used PNG image files. This is because PersonalJava 1.2 is only required to support a minimum set of image types (GIF, XBM, and JPEG). J2ME MIDP, on the other hand, is required at a minimum to support PNG images.

In the remote case, we use the J2SE version of the Wingfoot SOAP client. This version of the SOAP client has the same APIs, except for the transport used. Recall that in the Palm `SOAPClient` we used `HTTPTransport`, which underneath uses MIDP's GCF. PersonalJava is J2SE, and so it does not have

GCF. Wingfoot gets around this difference by providing a different transport class: J2SEHTTPTransport.

```
try {
   // Prepare the Envelope
   Envelope requestEnvelope = new Envelope();
   requestEnvelope.setBody("extension", ".jpeg");

   // Prepare the call
   Call call = new Call(requestEnvelope);
   call.setMethodName("getNames");
   call.setTargetObjectURI("ImageService");

   // Prepare the transport
   J2SEHTTPTransport transport =
      new J2SEHTTPTransport(SOAP_ENDPOINT, null);
   transport.getResponse(true);

   // Make the call
   Envelope responseEnvelope = call.invoke(transport);

   // Parse the response
   if (responseEnvelope != null) {
      if (responseEnvelope.isFaultGenerated()) {
         Fault f = responseEnvelope.getFault();
         System.out.println("Error: " + f.getFaultString());
      }
      else {
         Object[] parameter =
            (Object[])responseEnvelope.getParameter(0);
         String[] temp = new String[parameter.length];
         for (int i=0; i<parameter.length; i++)
            temp[i] = (String)parameter[i];
         files = temp;
      }
   }
}
catch (java.net.ConnectException e) {
   (new ImageDialog(this, "Error", "Could not connect to " +
      SOAP_ENDPOINT)).show();
}
catch (Exception e) {
   (new ImageDialog(this, "Error", e.toString())).show();
}
```

Note that the code is very similar to the Palm SOAPClient, except for the different transport class.

To retrieve a local image, we load a byte array from a file with the image name, and create an image:

```
FileInputStream fis = null;
try {
    // read the file into a byte array
    File imageFile = new File(LOCAL_DIRECTORY + "\\" + name);
    if (imageFile.exists()) {
        fis = new FileInputStream(imageFile);
        int length = fis.available();
        imageByteArray = new byte[length];
        fis.read(imageByteArray);
        imageCanvasDimension = imageCanvas.getSize();
        image = Toolkit.getDefaultToolkit().createImage(↵
          imageByteArray).getScaledInstance(↵
            -1, imageCanvasDimension.height, Image.SCALE_FAST);
        MediaTracker tracker = new MediaTracker(this);
        tracker.addImage(image,0);
        try {tracker.waitForID(0);} catch (InterruptedException e){};
    }
}
catch (Exception e) {
    (new ImageDialog(this, "Error", e.toString())).show();
}
finally {
    try { if (fis != null) fis.close(); } catch (Exception e) {}
}
```

Note the use of MediaTracker. Because createImage can spawn a separate thread to do its work, as it can take a long time to do some image tasks, we want to make sure that the task is finished before we go to the next step. This is done by using a MediaTracker that waits for a task with a given identifier (in this case, 0) to complete.

Again the code that retrieves an image from the ImageService Web service is quite familiar, except for the use of J2SEHTTPTransport:

```
try {
    // Prepare the Envelope
    Envelope requestEnvelope = new Envelope();
    requestEnvelope.setBody("name", name);

    // Prepare the call
    Call call = new Call(requestEnvelope);
    call.setMethodName("getImage");
```

```java
        call.setTargetObjectURI("ImageService");
        TypeMappingRegistry registry = new TypeMappingRegistry();
        registry.mapTypes("urn:BeanService", "ImageValue",
           new ImageValue().getClass(),
           new BeanSerializer().getClass(),
           new BeanSerializer().getClass());
        call.setMappingRegistry(registry);

        // Prepare the transport
        J2SEHTTPTransport transport =
           new J2SEHTTPTransport(SOAP_ENDPOINT, null);
        transport.getResponse(true);

        // Make the call
        Envelope responseEnvelope = call.invoke(transport);

        // Parse the response
        if (responseEnvelope != null) {
           if (responseEnvelope.isFaultGenerated()) {
              Fault f = responseEnvelope.getFault();
              System.out.println("Error: " + f.getFaultString());
           }
           else {
              ImageValue imageValue =
                 (ImageValue)responseEnvelope.getParameter(0);
              Date date =
                 new Date(imageValue.getDateAsLong().longValue());
              Base64 encodedImage =
                 new Base64(imageValue.getEncodedImage());
              imageByteArray = encodedImage.getBytes();
              imageCanvasDimension = imageCanvas.getSize();
              image =
                 Toolkit.getDefaultToolkit().createImage(
                 imageByteArray).getScaledInstance(-1,
                 imageCanvasDimension.height, Image.SCALE_FAST);
              MediaTracker tracker = new MediaTracker(this);
              tracker.addImage(image,0);
              try {tracker.waitForID(0);}
              catch (InterruptedException e){};
           }
        }
     }
     catch (Exception e) {
        (new ImageDialog(this, "Error", e.toString())).show();
     }
```

We can test the `ImageViewer` application on the desktop prior to deploying it to a PocketPC device. The Ant build target `TestImageViewer` performs this task:

```
<target name="TestImageViewer" depends="CompilePocketPC">
  <java
      classname="com.javaonpdas.webservices.clients.wingfoot.↵
ImageViewer"
      dir="."
      fork="true"
      failonerror="true">
     <classpath>
        <pathelement location="${pocketpclib}\$↵
{pocketpcsoaplib}"/>
        <pathelement location="${pocketpcdestination}↵
\pocketpc.jar"/>
     </classpath>
    <arg line=""/>
  </java>
</target>
```

To deploy the application to the PocketPC, we use the Ant target `Deploy-PocketPC`, which copies the `pocketpc.jar` to the PC's PocketPC synchronization folder.

```
<target name="DeployPocketPC" depends="CompilePocketPC">
  <copy file="${pocketpcdestination}\pocketpc.jar"
    todir="${pocketpcdeploy}" />
  <copy todir="${pocketpcdeploy}">
    <fileset dir="${pocketpclib}"/>
  </copy>
</target>
```

On starting the application, we see the frame as shown in Figure 8.17.

Selecting an image name retrieves the image from local storage and displays it on the screen, as shown in Figure 8.18.

Selecting the Remote button and selecting an image name retrieves that image from the `ImageService` Web service, and displays it on the screen, as shown in Figure 8.19.

Figure 8.17   The PocketPC version of ImageViewer, showing image names

Figure 8.18   The PocketPC version of ImageViewer, showing an image from local storage

Figure 8.19 The PocketPC version of ImageViewer, showing an image from remote storage

Summary

In this chapter we have explored using Web services to integrate a PDA application with the enterprise. For PDAs with more limited memory and processing capacity, we have seen that Web services are possible, but a preferable technique is to use a proxy on the server. The proxy does as much of the work as possible on the PDA's behalf, and exchanges information with the PDA using a very simple protocol.

For more powerful PDAs, such as the PocketPC, we can use SOAP directly to access server-side functionality.

CHAPTER 9

Futures

In this chapter we point out some emerging technologies and specifications relevant to Java on the Palm devices and the PocketPC.

Technologies

JXTA for J2ME

JXTA[1] is a Java-based technology for implementing dynamic peer-to-peer networks on mobile devices, PCs, and servers. An implementation of JXTA for J2ME devices is in the early stages of development, although it has been demonstrated on several devices.

Jini Surrogate Architecture

The Jini Surrogate Architecture and the IP Interconnect Specification provide a means for constrained devices to participate in Jini communities. Refer to http://developer.jini.org/exchange/projects/surrogate/overview.pdf for an overview.

---

1. Refer to http://www.jxta.org/.

Specifications

Java APIs for Bluetooth (JSR82)

This specification targets Java devices based on CLDC to provide access to Bluetooth connectivity. Refer to `http://www.jcp.org/jsr/detail/82.jsp`.

J2ME Web Services Specification (JSR172)

This specification aims to provide a standard Web service access API for CLDC-based devices. Refer to `http://www.jcp.org/jsr/detail/172.jsp`.

Location API for J2ME (JSR179)

This specification will provide a standard API for obtaining information about the device's physical location, and targets CLDC devices. Refer to `http://www.jcp.org/jsr/detail/179.jsp`.

Appendix A

Packages in CLDC

Table A.1 Packages in CLDC

java.lang	Classes	Boolean
		Byte
		Character
		Class
		Integer
		Long
		Math
		Object
		Runtime
		Short
		String
		StringBuffer
		System
		Thread
		Throwable
	Interfaces	Runnable

(continued)

Table A.1   Packages in CLDC *(Continued)*

	Exceptions	ArithmeticException
		ArrayIndexOutOfBoundsException
		ArrayStoreException
		ClassCastException
		ClassNotFoundException
		Exception
		IllegalAccessException
		IllegalArgumentException
		IllegalMonitorStateException
		IllegalThreadStateException
		IndexOutOfBoundsException
		InstantiationException
		InterruptedException
		NegativeArraySizeException
		NullPointerException
		NumberFormatException
		RuntimeException
		SecurityException
		StringIndexOutOfBoundsException
	Errors	Error
		OutOfMemoryError
		VirtualMachineError
java.io	Classes	ByteArrayInputStream
		ByteArrayOutputStream
		DataInputStream
		DataOutputStream
		InputStream
		InputStreamReader
		OutputStream
		OutputStreamWriter
		PrintStream
		Reader
		Writer
	Interfaces	DataInput
		DataOutput

(continued)

Table A.1 Packages in CLDC *(Continued)*

	Exceptions	EOFException
		InterruptedIOException
		IOException
		UnsupportedEncodingException
		UTFDataFormatException
	Errors	
java.util	Classes	Calendar
		Date
		Hashtable
		Random
		Stack
		TimeZone
		Vector
	Interfaces	Enumeration
	Exceptions	EmptyStackException
		NoSuchElementException
	Errors	
javax.microedition.io	Classes	Connector
	Interfaces	Connection
		ContentConnection
		Datagram
		DatagramConnection
		InputConnection
		OutputConnection
		StreamConnection
		StreamConnectionNotifier
	Exceptions	ConnectionNotFoundException
	Errors	

Appendix B

Extensions of CLDC Provided by MIDP

Table B.1   Extensions Provided by MIDP beyond CLDC

java.lang	Classes	None
	Interfaces	None
	Exceptions	IllegalStateException
	Errors	None
java.io	Classes	None
	Interfaces	None
	Exceptions	None
	Errors	None
java.util	Classes	Timer TimerTask
	Interfaces	None
	Exceptions	None
	Errors	None

(continued)

Table B.1   Extensions Provided by MIDP beyond CLDC *(Continued)*

javax.microedition.rms	Classes	RecordStore
	Interfaces	RecordComparator RecordEnumeration RecordFilter RecordListener
	Exceptions	InvalidRecordIDException RecordStoreException RecordStoreFullException RecordStoreNotFoundException RecordStoreNotOpenException
	Errors	None
javax.microedition.midlet	Classes	MIDlet
	Interfaces	None
	Exceptions	MIDletStateChangeException
	Errors	None
javax.microedition.io	Classes	None
	Interfaces	HttpConnection
	Exceptions	None
	Errors	None

(continued)

Table B.1   Extensions Provided by MIDP beyond CLDC *(Continued)*

javax.microedition.lcdui	Classes	Alert
		AlertType
		Canvas
		ChoiceGroup
		Command
		DateField
		Display
		Displayable
		Font
		Form
		Gauge
		Graphics
		Image
		ImageItem
		Item
		List
		Screen
		StringItem
		TextBox
		TextField
		Ticker
	Interfaces	Choice
		CommandListener
		ItemStateListener
	Exceptions	None
	Errors	None

Appendix C

Jeode -D Properties

This appendix describes the properties you can set to alter JeodeRuntime jeode.evm.memory settings.[1]

> jeode.evm.memory.compaction[2]
> jeode.evm.memory.size
> jeode.evm.memory.overallSize
> jeode.evm.memory.sysLimit
> jeode.evm.memory.sysStart
> jeode.evm.memory.sysExtend
> jeode.evm.memory.javaLimit
> jeode.evm.memory.javaStart
> jeode.evm.memory.javaExtend
> jeode.evm.memory.stackSize
> jeode.evm.memory.stackOverflowZone

---

1. Reproduced with permission from Insignia Solutions.
2. Denotes a property group.

jeode.evm.memory.size   The overall amount of memory in the target machine, in bytes

> Type: String
> Default Value: 16 m

This property value is not used directly by the EVM, but is used to define appropriate default values for the following other types of memory properties:

- jeode.evm.memory.overallSize
- jeode.evm.memory.sysLimit
- jeode.evm.memory.javaLimit
- jeode.evm.memory.stackSize
- jeode.evm.compiler.ehSize
- jeode.evm.compiler.dataSize
- jeode.evm.compiler.codeBuffTotal

These default values represent Insignia's estimate of optimal generic settings for performance, based on this overall memory size. You can then alter these default values as required for your specific application and device.

jeode.evm.memory.overallSize   The maximum amount of dynamic Java/System memory allowed

> Type: Integer
> Default Value: 15 m
> Must be positive

This is the maximum amount of dynamic memory (in bytes) allowed at run-time for Java objects and EVM data—also see notes for stack size. Dynamic memory use is that determined by JeodeRuntime at run-time, satisfied by dynamic memory allocation requests upon the target OS.

The dynamic memory acquired by JeodeRuntime is shared between:

- Java memory: relocatable, garbage collectable Java heap objects
- System memory: immovable Jeode "system" objects

Normally, either of these could (theoretically) occupy the whole of the dynamically allocated memory if run-time conditions required. You can also use the jeode.evm.memory.javaLimit and jeode.evm.memory.sysLimit properties to define ceiling values for Java or system memory usage if needed.

Note: To find static memory use (including the space occupied by the Jeode EVM executable and its predefined data structures), run a target-specific executable analyzer tool on your host (for example, `objdump`).

jeode.evm.memory.sysLimit   When nonzero, puts a limit on memory used for EVM data

>   Type: Integer
>   Default Value: 0
>   Must be positive

This defines the maximum amount of dynamic memory to allocate to Jeode system objects, in bytes. System memory is part of dynamic memory, and shares (with the Java heap) the area determined by Maximum dynamic memory size. The default is zero (unlimited), which means that the only limit is that set by Maximum dynamic memory size—usage is determined at run-time as required.

jeode.evm.memory.sysStart   Initial size of system memory

>   Type: Integer
>   Default Value: 32 k
>   Must be positive

This defines how much memory is granted to the system heap when the EVM starts, and the overall commitment will never drop below this level.

jeode.evm.memory.sysExtend   How much to grow system memory by

>   Type: Integer
>   Default Value: 32 k
>   Must be positive

This provides a hint to the EVM about how much to extend the EVM data memory when it is necessary. When the region is grown the EVM will try to ensure that approximately this much is available without having to grow it again.

jeode.evm.memory.javaLimit   When nonzero, puts a limit on memory used for Java objects

>   Type: Integer
>   Default Value: 0
>   Must be positive

This defines the maximum amount of dynamic memory to allocate to Java heap, in bytes. As part of dynamic memory, the heap shares (with system memory) the area determined by Maximum dynamic memory size. The default is zero (unlimited), which means that the only limit is that set by Maximum dynamic memory size—usage is determined at run-time as required.

jeode.evm.memory.javaStart   How much memory to grant to the Java heap on startup

> Type: Integer
> Default Value: 32 k
> Must be positive

This defines how much memory is granted to the Java heap when the EVM starts, and the overall commitment will never drop below this level.

jeode.evm.memory.javaExtend   How much to grow Java memory region by

> Type: Integer
> Default Value: 32 k
> Must be positive

This provides a hint to the EVM about how much to extend Java object memory when it is necessary. When the Java heap is grown the EVM will try to ensure that approximately this much is available without having to grow the heap again.

jeode.evm.memory.stackSize   The maximum size of any one thread's stack in bytes

> Type: Integer
> Default Value: 64 k
> Must be positive

This is the maximum stack size requested from the target OS for each JeodeRuntime thread (including any Java threads), in bytes. As your Java application may be multi-threaded, the total memory requirement clearly depends on the maximum number of simultaneously active threads.

JeodeMonitor shows the threads running in your application, and their total stack usage. Some OSs (for example, WinNT and WinCE) will effectively ignore this limit, and automatically increase stack sizes as the application requires up to a hard-coded limit defined at link-time.

For all Windows targets, you should not increase the stack size beyond the limit set at link-time—if you do exceed this limit, the EVM's behavior is undefined. For the supplied JeodeRuntime executable binaries on Windows platforms, these limits are:

- For CE 2.12/x86: 128 K
- For Windows NT: 1 Mb
- For all other CE platforms (including CE 3.00): 64 K

For some OSs (for example, SnapOS), this memory comes from the pool whose size is bounded by Maximum dynamic memory size. For other targets (for example, Linux and VxWorks), this memory is obtained directly from the target OS. This is because some target OSs allocate memory for thread stacks internally, and do not allow JeodeRuntime separately to allocate this memory.

jeode.evm.memory.stackOverflowZone   Size of the stack overflow zone

Type: Integer
Default Value: 16 k
Must be positive

When a thread enters this zone, a stack overflow exception will be thrown.This needs to be less than the stack size setting. A value of zero indicates that stack overflow checks should not be performed.

Appendix D

Jeode -X Options

This appendix[1] describes EVM-specific command-line options, which are prefixed by -X[option].

To display options specific to the Jeode EVM, use the -X option.

-X
-X@:
-Xdebug
-Xlinenum
-Xms
-Xmx
-Xnoclassgc
-Xnoprogressbar
-Xnoverify
-Xoss
-Xprofile
-Xrun
-Xrunjdwp
-Xss
-Xverify
-Xverifyremote
-Xversion
-Xwinceconsole / -Xnowinceconsole

---

1. Reproduced with permission from Insignia Solutions.

-X

Displays help for non-standard options. Standard EVM options are displayed with the -? option.

-X@:<filename>

Use a set of property values defined in a configuration file (a .evm file) to configure EVM run-time properties. See the properties documentation for more information.

Note: On Windows CE targets, the <filename> must be a full path name, even if the .evm file is in the same \Windows folder as the EVM executable.

-Xdebug

This option enables the JVMDI debugging subsystem.

-Xlinenum

This option keeps the line number information in any loaded classfiles, so a stack backtrace will show line numbers rather than bytecode offsets. When -Xdebug or -Xprofile options are used they automatically include the line number tables.

When an exception is thrown and the stack trace is printed on the console, the EVM shows both file names and line numbers.

-Xms

As for -ms

-Xmx

As for -mx

-Xnoclassgc

As for -noclassgc

-Xnoprogressbar

This option suppresses display of the loading progress bar that appears when the EVM is being first loaded (for Windows CE target platforms only).

-Xnoverify

As for -noverify

-Xoss

As for -oss

-Xprofile

This option enables the JVMPI profiling subsystem.

-Xrun

Format:

```
-Xrun<module>[:<options>]
```

This option dynamically loads a library module that extends the functionality of the EVM, where module specifies the library module to load, and options specifies the module specific options (if any).

-Xrunjdwp

This option enables the JDWP/JDI debugging subsystem for the connection of a remote debugger.

-Xss

As for -ss

-Xverify

As for -verify

-Xverifyremote

As for -verifyremote

-Xversion

As for -version

-Xwinceconsole and -Xnowinceconsole (Windows CE targets only)

Use the -Xwinceconsole option to enable the EVM console on Windows CE targets (this is the default behavior). Use the -Xnowinceconsole option to disable the EVM console on Windows CE targets. These options are only available on Windows CE EVMs.

Appendix E

JDK 1.1.8 Demonstrations on PersonalJava 1.2

Table E.1 lists the results of testing when each of the demonstrations—included with JDK 1.1.8—is run on PersonalJava 1.2. In the left-hand column, the name of the demonstration is listed. In the right-hand column, an indication of whether the demonstration works in the same way on PersonalJava 1.2 as it does on JDK 1.1.8 is listed. The intention is to give an indication of overall compatibility.

Table E.1   Running the JDK 1.1.8 Demonstrations on PersonalJava 1.2

Animator	
example 1	No—no animation
example 2	No—no animation
example 3	No—"Loading images - please wait"—no animation
example 4	Yes
ArcTest	Yes

(continued)

Table E.1   Running the JDK 1.1.8 Demonstrations on PersonalJava 1.2   *(Continued)*

awt-1.1	
Lightweight Components	
Round Button	No—"Couldn't find applet: actual.ExampleApplet"
Openlook Button	No—"Couldn't find applet: actual.ExampleApplet"
Spinner	No—"Couldn't find applet: actual.ExampleApplet"
Gauge	No—"Couldn't find applet: actual.ExampleApplet"
Event Examples	
Anonymous Classes	Yes
Static Nested Class	Yes
Redispatching	Yes
Complete Example	Yes
Unicode	Yes
BarChart	Yes
Blink	Yes
CardTest	Yes
Clock	Yes
DitherTest	Yes
DrawTest	Yes
Fractal	Yes
GraphicsTest	Yes
GraphLayout	
example 1	Yes
example 2	Yes
example 3	Yes
example 4	Yes

(continued)

Table E.1 Running the JDK 1.1.8 Demonstrations on PersonalJava 1.2 *(Continued)*

i18n	
Collate	Yes
DateTimeFormat	Yes
MessageFormat	Yes
NumberFormat	Yes
TextBound	Yes
ImageMap	Yes
JumpingBox	Yes
MoleculeViewer	
example 1	No—"Error in model: java.security.AccessControlException: access denied"
example 2	No—"Error in model: java.security.AccessControlException: access denied"
example 3	No—"Error in model: java.security.Acc"
NervousTest	Yes
SimpleGraph	Yes
SortDemo	Yes
SpreadSheet	Yes
TicTacToe	Yes
WireFrame	
example 1	No—"Error in model: java.security.Acc"
example 2	No—"Error in model: java.security.AccessControlException: access denied"
example 3	No—"Error in model: java.security.AccessControlException: access denied"
example 4	No—"Error in model: java.security.AccessControlException: access denied"

Index

Available in September, 2003

CINDY BLOCH
ANNETTE WAGNER

MIDP 2.0
STYLE GUIDE

MIDP (Mobile Information Device Profile) responds to industry needs for increased gaming, multimedia, and security features, and is widely regarded as the platform of choice for mobile applications. The completely revised MIDP 2.0 is essential for Java developers seeking to create exciting and easy-to-use mobile games for the consumer market.

Of the many challenges facing developers, ensuring that the design, development, and construction of the user-interface (UI) is a top priority. Developers must focus on usability, as few consumer-oriented phone users will find rebooting their phone to be an acceptable practice. This book provides a set of clear and concise guidelines for creating Java applications for wireless devices and includes visual examples of what developers should and should *not* do when creating these complex and interactive mobile applications.

©2003, PAPER, 304 PAGES, 0-321-19801-8, $39.99

ABOUT THE AUTHOR

ANNETTE WAGNER is currently the human interface lead for the Java 2 Micro Edition Platform™ in the Java Software division of Sun Microsystems, Inc. For the last several years she has been working on designing and building Java technologies that are used in cell phones, two-way pagers, PDAs, screen phones, and TVs. Cindy Bloch writes technical documentation for Sun Microsystems' Java Software division.